ETHEREUM IN A NUTSHELL

THE DEFINITIVE GUIDE TO INTRODUCE YOU TO THE WORLD OF ETHEREUM, CRYPTOCURRENCIES, SMART CONTRACTS AND MASTER IT COMPLETELY

SEBASTIAN ACEVEDO

WB PUBLISHING

CONTENTS

HOW TO USE THE BOOK

How to use the book

First of all I would like to thank you for your trust and for choosing me as your guide to embark on this journey into the world of Cryptocurrencies. This book will help you to understand and master this world with the objective of obtaining an excellent financial education through the comprehension and understanding of Cryptocurrencies. In this book we will go from the most basic to the most advanced.

We understand that entering the world of cryptocurrencies can be tedious and very slow because there is a lot of information that we must understand and assimilate, usually the pioneers in this type of technology are people who have no problem to generate passive income online because they have some basic knowledge of this world that can help them a lot. The purpose of this book is that you can also shorten this path and have the knowledge in time to take advantage of them, as you know the world of cryptocurrencies moves very quickly and you can not waste time.

This technology is here to stay and to give us, the ordinary people, more economic and financial freedom.

In my experience, one of the things that caught my attention when I became interested in cryptocurrencies back in 2011, was the concept of freedom that is related to currencies such as Bitcoin, Monero, Dash, Zcash, etc. where the control of the whole process always goes by hand with the user because of the privacy they provide. Don't worry, you will understand these concepts later on during the development of the book.

In this book I will teach you the different approaches to Cryptocurrencies and the technology behind it: starting from the actual concept of money to the Blockchain, why it works, what is the secret behind it and we will also debunk some myths related to some concepts.

The objective of this book is to teach you to have a more complete and complex notion about Cryptocurrencies, from the most basic concepts such as knowing how everything works, how the pieces fit together, to the most advanced.

I have also taken the time to suggest some resources to get you started on the right foot. Keep in mind that many of these links are affiliate links, so you will receive some discounts and benefits by using the referred link, at no cost to you. So take advantage of it.

I wrote this book not only to inform you about the world of cryptocurrencies but also to motivate you to take that step that is so hard for you and take action, that is why I want to ask you one thing, do not give up throughout this book, follow the advice at your own risk, I promise you that by finishing this book and applying step by step my advice and teachings you will be able to better understand this world and according to your personal actions achieve financial freedom or also support this initiative that gives power to us citizens against the current financial system that is too manipulated and makes a few people rich.

Again, thank you very much for purchasing this book, I hope you enjoy it.

FIRST EDITION

ABOUT ME

Why should you listen to me?

Greetings, my name is Sebastian Andres, I am an entrepreneur, writer and world traveler. I am a cryptocurrency enthusiast since 2011 when I started to get interested in this world. I feel extremely blessed to have been born in this era, and to be able to experience the growth of these technologies such as the internet and cryptocurrencies.

For more than 10 years I have focused on developing several internet businesses, which taught me to develop my own strategies and methods to generate passive income. Cryptocurrencies was one of them and that is how I achieved financial freedom.

The purpose of my books, more specifically of the collection "Cryptocurrency Basics" (in which I bring the most current and reliable information on cryptocurrencies, if you are interested you can look for the other books in this collection, in which we address other cryptos) is to be a source of inspiration for you and generate a change in those who are not satisfied with the established and know that they can give more, that they can generate a positive change in their lives and get to design that lifestyle they want so much.

I am confident that this information will help you to get that final jump start and get into cryptocurrencies in depth.

DISCLAIMER

Important

Investing in financial markets such as cryptocurrencies and other assets can lead to money losses. The purpose of this book is only educational and does not represent an investment advice, for that there are already many professionals in the area that can help you. Proceed with caution, at your own risk and remember, never invest more than you are willing to lose.

By continuing to read this book you accept this Warning.

ONE

UNDERSTANDING THE LOGIC BEHIND ETHEREUM

Let's start by saying that Ethereum is a digital platform linked to the Blockchain (technological system that allows to manage in a personalized, decentralized, synchronized and secure way, all the information of records and movements generated by computer terminals and other devices), and that expands its use to a wide range of applications in the online network.

Ether (ETH) is the native cryptocurrency of Ethereum, and is recognized as the second largest and most powerful virtual currency in the world after Bitcoin. Therefore, from now on we will be able to clearly identify that Ethereum is the platform and Ether is the cryptocurrency, product of the ingenuity that two young people visualized and established themselves in the world as public, real, physical and identifiable figures.

Knowing that you have started this fascinating reading, and you are looking to become part of an interesting and really productive journey in the cosmos of cryptocurrencies, let's take a look at the origins and foundations that inspired and made possible the creation of Ethereum.

Ethereum is a platform for unmonitored decentralized applications, which is gaining importance, value and recognition day by day; which make it appear as a tool and resource of financial interest, to the point that renowned banking institutions such as UBS of Switzerland, BNP Paribas of France and Barclays of the United Kingdom, among others; see in Ethereum solidity and prestige, far above what has been currently representing traditional money.

THE ORIGINS of Ethereum date back to the end of 2013. By then, two young enthusiasts and entrepreneurs embarked on a demanding project, with great characteristics of new demand and actuality, with an infinity of structural details and the feasibility of being able to create it, consolidating a contemporary financial concept that would permeate with a decisive turn all personal, corporate and global economies; a positive and encouraging turn.

In 2014, the Ethereum project was formally presented for the first time, and by 2015 it was able to finalize its programming, preparation and design phase, definitively making its way and establishing itself in the modern spectrum of crypto assets.

Ethereum was created by the Englishman Gavin Wood and the Russian-Canadian Vitálik Buterin, when the latter was only 21 years old. We can take it for granted that the history and origins of Ethereum date back to 2011.

At that time, Vitálik Buterin was 17 years old and was starting as a Bitcoin employee, working as a programmer. Seeing certain and certain flaws in the Bitcoin platform and some operational deficiencies, Buterin decided to undertake the creation of Ethereum and develop a Blockchain technology superior to the one currently implemented, known and managed by his employer.

BUTERIN CONSIDERED that Bitcoin does not work directly or correctly on the setbacks that arose, he believed that only individual applications were sought, a fact that inspires him to abandon Bitcoin to devote time, effort and creativity in favor of his own project:

THE ETHEREUM PLATFORM.

Currently, the active development of Ethereum is operated by the Ethereum Foundation, a non-profit, non-governmental organization founded in 2014 and dedicated to extending and expanding the development of Ethereum as a technology platform for the benefit of the global community.

IT IS important to emphasize and reiterate that Ethereum itself is neither a cryptocurrency nor an open source protocol for the realization of payment programs; it is a platform for the effective operation of decentralized applications, from which the operating systems of various functions and multiple alternatives are executed on the network.

All this happens from what we could call its nerve center, thanks to a powerful virtual machine known as Ethereum Virtual Machine (EVM).

For this reason it is valid to say that Ethereum is an operating system, distributed through an extensive network and very distant from other systems or platforms; it is 100% decentralized, collaborative and is not governed or regulated by the tutelage, direction or management of any governmental, financial or commercial entity.About to turn 6 years old, the Ethereum platform has experienced since its virtual currency Ether; ups and downs of outstanding importance, highlighting the experience lived at the beginning of 2020 when its value went from $130 to $285 in mid-February. This situation, which later and due to fears of investing after the COVID-19 pandemic, led Ether to a downward peak in just one week, closing at $107 on March 12.

TODAY and just as we write this paper, Ether is in a privileged position holding its second rung as the world's most powerful cryptocurrency, trading above $4,012.00 as of May 13, 2021. If we consider that two months after its launch, on September 30, 2015 the value was set at $0.71, within a year it reached $13.22 and a year later at $1,351.00 on January 14, 2018.

Its uptrend was noted with the boom of cryptocurrencies in 2017 to then begin a decline that made it reach $199.26 from which we have seen a historic recovery that foresees an interesting and very encouraging future for the global and full structure of the Ethereum ecosystem.

IN RECENT YEARS Ethereum continues to gain great popularity within the crypto system and world, based on its strength and figure as a stable, secure, independent multifunctional platform. It is backed in its developments by the Ethereum Foundation and the position of Ether, its native currency, supported by its powerful Ethereum Virtual Machine (EVM). It is worth emphasizing that Ethereum, as an open source software project driven by its community, has evolved and is still successfully driven since its inception and continues to grow.

THE ERA of cryptocurrencies saw the light of day with the appearance of the first virtual option, when in 2009 Bitcoin opened an alternative to physical money. Since then and to this day, there are already more than 7,000 cryptocurrencies that seek to somehow lead the market, offering their best structure and becoming a safe and reliable financial tool. By empowering their designs and reinforcing their programs, activating feasible operating systems for a guaranteed negotiation. All this and much more is part of the development within the Ethereum platform, which has transformed the way of hosting applications and proposing a cutting-edge financial instrument.

VITÁLIK BUTERIN, born in Kolomna, Russia, on January 31, 1994. Web developer, cryptoactivist and also co-founder of Bitcoin Magazine, experienced innovator in various digital projects, researcher and analyst; who has managed to become for his young age one of the most influential and inspiring people for his great contribution to the construction of the cryptogalaxy, is the creator of the ambitious Ethereum project, which in just over 5 years already adopts 14 million subscribers and every day grows in confidence.

Buterin somehow and from a very young age enjoyed an intrinsic magic. Fanatic and assiduous player "hooked" to the video game World Of Warcraft; he enjoyed a full time between 2007 and 2010, after devoting hours to the game, seeking to climb positions and climb from level to level as a wizard, which Vitálik himself considers as of valuable repercussion in his future research and creation of Ethereum.

A DECISIVE EVENT marked this great transition, when the company Blizzard, owner of the game World Of Warcraft, made changes in the parameters that affected one of Vitálik's characters.

What happened precisely was that the update made to the game eliminated the Siphon Life Spell that he used on his witch character.

According to his testimony, that experience allowed him to see what he considered the negative side of centralized development systems.

It was incomprehensible for him to accept and see how the game's virtual platform took away what, after days and seasons of recreational activity, had cost him so much effort to build.

Brief description of the functioning of the Ethereum Blockchain and the organization of the blocks Let's start this section by defining what Blockchain is, as its term translated from English says, it is a Blockchain, it is a single record, agreed and distributed in various nodes or spaces where several points of a network converge. In relation to cryptocurrencies, we could compare it to a ledger in which all the transactions of a company or organization are recorded.

ITS OPERATION COULD PERHAPS BE complex to understand if we delve into the internal aspects of its configuration. However, the basic idea is quite simple and practical to understand.

EACH OF THE BLOCKS STORES:

- A CERTAIN NUMBER of records or valid transactions.
    - Information inherent to the block.

- THE LINKAGE with the previous and next block through the Hash, a cryptographic operation that generates unique and unrepeatable identifiers for each block, a code of its own, which would be like the fingerprint of that block.

CONSEQUENTLY, each block will have a specific, unique and immovable place within the chain, as each block will contain information from the hash generated in the block that precedes it. The closure of the chain is stored in each node of the network that will constitute the Blockchain, providing in turn an exact copy of the chain to all members of the network.

AS NEW RECORDS ARE CREATED, they are initially verified and validated by the network nodes and subsequently incorporated into a new blockchain that will be linked to the chain.

ETHEREUM'S OPERATION corresponds to an open source platform based on the Blockchain technology described above. This blockchain is hosted on a large number of computers distributed around the world, which guarantees its decentralized quality. Each of these computers has a copy of the Blockchain and must apply a generalized agreement or consensus prior to the implementation of any change in the network.

Ethereum's Blockchain is closely related to Bitcoin's, in that it is a record of the history of transactions made. However, developers have the power to build and deploy decentralized software and applications or "DApps" (Decentralized Applications) whose operation is based on a decentralized network, with the Ethereum network. These likewise are stored on the Blockchain along with the transaction log.

AS MENTIONED ABOVE, Ethereum is based on the same Bitcoin protocol and its blockchain design, properly configured so that applications and operations beyond money systems can be supported. There is only one real similarity between the two Blockchains and that is that they both store and collect the total transaction history of their corresponding networks.

. . .

HOWEVER, it should be noted that the Ethereum Blockchain has an activity that goes much further, doing a little more than just storing. In addition to archiving the transaction history, each of the nodes of the Ethereum network or platform also needs to download the most recent status or current information of each smart contract (Smart Contract, which we will see later), the balance or credit of each user and the complete smart contract code and where it is stored.

In essence, the Ethereum Blockchain can be described as a powerful state machine with a strict foundation in its transactions. From a computing point of view or environment, a state machine is defined as something with the ability to read and display a whole series of inputs and transact to a new state based on those inputs.

When these operations or transactions are executed, the machine transitions to another state.

EACH OF ETHEREUM'S states is made up of millions of transactions, these transactions are grouped together to give rise to a block and thus generate a chain with each and every one of the blocks previously formed and linked together. In order for the transaction to be finally incorporated into the ledger, it must be validated and duly undergo the mining process.

Mining is the process through which a certain number of nodes apply all their computing power and capacity to complete the Proof Of Work (PoW), which is essentially a mathematical puzzle.

The more powerful and efficient the computer is, the faster the puzzle can be solved and put together. An accurate answer to this puzzle is itself a Proof of Work, which guarantees the validity and confirmation of a block.

THERE ARE many miners in all corners of the world who are in constant competition with each other to try to create and validate a new block, since each time one is given; new Ether tokens (unit of value created by an organization to manage its own business models) are generated, which go to the hands of that miner. Miners are the backbone of the Ethereum platform, since their important function of confirming and validating transactions and any other type of activity within the network allows them the possibility of generating new tokens.

LET us always keep in mind and it is worth remembering that the Blockchain technology is, if you will; inspired by the concept of Distributed Ledger (DLT), which has as its technical foundation a networked system of computers that are guided by the peer-to-peer network principle.

The contributions for the creation and validation of consensus are referred to cryptographic processes or game theory.

THE CONCEPT of Distributed Ledger (DLT) or Distributed Ledger Technology (DLT) refers to a Decentralized Public Registry. All the information contained in such a ledger usually reflects a whole chain of transaction data that testifies to account movements. A network or set of computers supports in group form all the information and each node of the network has a copy or replica of this conglomerate of data.

LET'S look at the situation with an example:

WHEN, through the support of a Blockchain application Luis makes a transfer to Nancy for the payment of a watch, the operation or transaction is recorded in a distributed ledger. Immediately, all members of the application will be able to track and view it.

. . .

IN BLOCKCHAIN NETWORKS AND PLATFORMS, virtual currencies such as Bitcoin, Dash, Ether, etc. are used instead of fiat or traditional money.

The idea of Distributed Ledger has its foundations in Peer To Peer (P2P) networks, since, in this way communication between computers in the same range and network is facilitated.

IN BLOCKCHAIN PEER-TO-PEER NETWORKS, virtual values are not transmitted directly from one point to another, instead, all participants, who to interact with the Blockchain must have a client software that systematizes the entire process of consensus as the copy of the information status; they all have a replica of each and every one of the transactions that they store in an incognito way, from where it is broken down who holds what value and at what time.

When there is any change in the status of the data, each replica of each of the acting nodes matches the previous version of the Blockchain.

For a change in the main database to be accepted, all computers constituting the network are obliged to determine by majority that the reforms are genuine. This means that only if the majority of the participating nodes accept the modifications, they will have to be accepted by all the members of the network.

If, on the other hand, at least half plus one of the nodes determine that the changes are not genuine, all members of the network must reject them.

This situation can occur when, for example, the new data refutes previous replicas to the blockchain. For this reason, when any of the nodes needs to make changes or modifications to the Blockchain, it must demonstrate and prove that it is duly authorized to do so.

. . .

UNDERSTANDING **the Blockchain technology behind the workings of Ethereum**

BLOCKCHAIN, sometimes referred to as distributed ledger technology (DLT), makes the history of any digital asset unalterable and transparent through the use of decentralization and cryptographic hashing.

A SIMPLE ANALOGY TO understand Blockchain technology is a Google document.

When we create a document and share it with a group of people, the document is distributed rather than copied or transferred. This creates a decentralized distribution chain that gives everyone access to the document at the same time. No one is locked out waiting for changes from another party, while all modifications to the document are recorded in real time, making changes completely transparent.

OF COURSE, Blockchain is much more complicated than a Google Doc, but the analogy is apt because it illustrates for us five critical ideas of the technology:

- A BLOCKCHAIN BLOCKCHAIN is a database that stores encrypted blocks of data and then chains them together to form a single chronological source of truth for the data.

- DIGITAL ASSETS ARE DISTRIBUTED RATHER than copied or transferred, creating an immutable record of an asset.
   - The asset is decentralized, allowing full real-time access and transparency to the public.

. . .

- A TRANSPARENT LEDGER of changes preserves the integrity of the document, creating confidence in the asset.

- BLOCKCHAIN'S inherent security measures and public ledger make it a prime technology for nearly every industry.

Blockchain is an especially promising and revolutionary technology because it helps reduce risk, eliminates fraud and provides transparency in a scalable way for countless uses.

HOW DOES BLOCKCHAIN WORK?

THE GOAL of using a blockchain is to allow people, particularly people who do not trust each other, to share valuable data in a secure and tamper-proof way.

BLOCKCHAIN CONSISTS of three important concepts: blocks, miners and nodes.

Blocks

EACH CHAIN CONSISTS of several blocks and each block has three basic elements:

The block data.

. . .

A 32-BIT INTEGER CALLED A NONCE. The nonce is randomly generated when a block is created, which then generates a block header hash.

THE HASH IS a 256-bit number attached to the nonce. It must start with a large number of zeros (i.e., be extremely small).

When the first block of a chain is created, a nonce generates the cryptographic hash. The data in the block is considered signed and forever bound to the nonce and hash unless it is extracted.

MINERS

MINERS CREATE new blocks on the chain through a process called mining.

IN A BLOCKCHAIN, each block has its own unique value and hash, but it also references the hash of the previous block in the chain, so mining a block is not easy, especially on large chains.

Miners use special software to solve the incredibly complex mathematical problem of finding a nonce that generates an accepted hash. Because the nonce is only 32 bits and the hash is 256, there are approximately four billion possible nonce-hash combinations that must be extracted before the correct one is found. When that happens, the miners are said to have found the "golden nonce" and their block is added to the chain.

Making a change to any block at the beginning of the chain requires re-mining not only the block with the change, but all the blocks that come after it. This is why it is extremely difficult to tamper with Blockchain technology. Think of it as "security in mathematics," as finding gold nonces requires an enormous amount of time and computing power.

WHEN A BLOCK IS SUCCESSFULLY MINED, the exchange is accepted by all nodes in the network and the miner is rewarded financially.

Nodes

One of the most important concepts of Blockchain technology is decentralization. No computer or organization can own the chain. Instead, it is a distributed ledger across nodes connected to the chain.

Nodes can be any type of electronic device that maintains copies of the blockchain and keeps the network running.

Each node has its own copy of the blockchain and the network must algorithmically approve any newly mined block for the chain to be updated, trusted and verified. Because blockchains are transparent, every share on the ledger can be easily verified and viewed. Each participant receives a unique alphanumeric identification number that shows their transactions.

The combination of public information with a system of checks and balances helps the blockchain maintain integrity and builds trust among users. Essentially, blockchain can be thought of as the scalability of trust through technology.

Through the Ether cryptocurrency, native to Ethereum, the highest percentages of transactions and negotiations of the already known NTF (Non Fungible Tokens), unique fashionable digital assets that are equivalent to virtual certificates of authenticity verified by means of the Blockchain, are carried out worldwide. One of the many causes affecting the rise in the price of Ether.

The beginning of May 2021 represented for Ethereum a historic moment, breaking a record mark for its value, reaching in such a short time of existence to exceed the barrier of $ 3,000.00 per Ether.

The impact did not remain silent among those who make life in the crypto world, as the fact became a trend in blogs and social networks throughout the network.

ETHER IS the second largest cryptocurrency in the digital financial system and currently represents a market value of over $387 billion. Its mother platform, Ethereum, its development center Ethereum Foundation, its dedicated operating system together with the role played by Ethereum Virtual Machine (EVM) and the meticulously structured design of its blockchain, make Ethereum a figure of representative security and trust among its users and future prospects.

Ethereum runs on open source operating software with features similar to those used by Bitcoin. We reiterate and insist on emphasizing that its operations are totally decentralized and unmonitored and create a kind of public ledger where each and every transaction is recorded, validated and confirmed. This technological dynamic is known as blockchain or Blockchain.

WHEN WE TALK ABOUT DECENTRALIZED, we mean that each of the participants can confirm the transactions, without the intervention of any governmental entity, local authority, federal bank or financial institution. This means, for example, that there is no need to wait for the approval of the central bank to issue an order, process the transaction and deliver a certain amount of printed money in physical form.

COMPARED to the technology behind Bitcoin, the verification of transactions within the Ethereum Blockchain takes only seconds, not minutes, and is therefore much faster. Another differentiating element is that Ethereum software was conceived with the idea of being used in other types of operations, such as art auctions, one of the most active uses today.

THE ETHEREUM BLOCKCHAIN has become the most widely used blockchain today, due to the growth of stablecoin and the rise of DeFi (Decentralized Finance).

Lately the price of Bitcoin has been trading in a moderately linear range and its trading volume has been staying relatively flat.

A SIGNIFICANT NUMBER of tokens on the Ethereum network have been on top of the price charts, most notably Decentralized Finance or DeFi tokens.

Recent data has reported that Ethereum has surpassed Bitcoin as the most liquid network in value per day. This means that the dollar value of Ether ETH transactions and tokens is higher than that of Bitcoin.

THE DECENTRALIZED FINANCE sector continues to gain popularity, all thanks to the stablecoins transactions that have impacted largely thanks to the notoriety of the DeFi, managing to settle in the course of the year 2020 much more than 508 million dollars. A figure that exceeds by 100% the amounts settled for the year 2019, when these reached the figure of 253 million dollars.

Bitcoin offers the market cryptocurrencies that operate through the Counterparty and Omni protocols, but these assets languish when compared to the capabilities of the Smart Contracts or smart contracts of the Ethereum network that continues to figure through the new possibilities of DeFi.

In conjunction with lower fees and faster times per transaction, Ethereum positions itself as the chain of choice for stable centralized and decentralized currencies.

USDT (Tether) was first exposed on the Bitcoin Blockchain, and currently only 13.2% of its supply resides on this cryptocurrency, while on the other hand 59.8% of USDT supply is hosted on the Ethereum Blockchain. For this reason, and because most of the USDT (Tether) balance is held on the Ethereum platform, Ethereum is the largest consumer of gas (unit of measurement to be discussed later) on the platform.

WITHOUT ANY DOUBT OR DISCUSSION, the Ethereum Blockchain is the most famous and popular in the industry. It is a distributed public network dedicated to running and developing programming code for decentralized applications and operating systems. In other words, it is a software that acts as a shared platform for all kinds of information and online resources. Moreover, such data cannot be modified and cannot be manipulated.

ETHEREUM'S BLOCKCHAIN could be considered similar enough to that of Bitcoin, however, there are certain differentiating elements. One of them is its programming language that allows its developers to produce software through which it is feasible to manage or process transactions, and likewise automate certain and certain results, something known as Smart Contracts, which will be developed later on.

However, in the context of the Blockchain it is appropriate to say that Smart Contracts ensure that the conditions, guidelines and terms established and agreed in a relationship are fully complied with. These contracts are covered by programs that are automatically executed as soon as the predefined conditions are met. The typical delays and costs involved in the development of manual agreements are set aside during the process.

. . .

THE STRUCTURE so well elaborated in the Ethereum Blockchain, besides giving life to its excellent Smart Contracts, which with their appearance have helped to proliferate this type of tools, not only in the cryptographic ecosystem, but outside it; it has also been ideal for developing the so-called DApps, Decentralized Applications that operate from a decentralized network. These resources give their users the possibility of accessing a wide range of different services in a totally secure way.

IN VERY PRECISE and general lines, the innovative alternatives offered by the Ethereum Blockchain are the same ones that catapulted the great fame of this powerful platform.

THESE FEATURES, together with its form, structure, benefits and novelties, are what have driven a large number of developers and programmers to use and understand the cutting-edge Blockchain technology behind Ethereum's operation.

ETHEREUM USE CASES

IN TERMS of crypto market positioning, Ethereum as a platform and its native virtual currency Ether maintain an undisputed and well-deserved second place as the most important cryptocurrency in the world, despite the fact that many users, subscribers and followers wonder why it has not become the first, because, considering among many reasons the undisputed effectiveness of its smart contracts, all its functions are always well weighted.

. . .

WE MUST BE honest in recognizing that Bitcoin leads and commands the smart contract sector, but it is Ethereum that executes and manages them in a much simpler way, a condition highlighted and valued by Buterin, its founder, who affirms its advanced scripting capabilities (ability to process commands that the system interprets and can execute) and the completeness of its structure.

ETHEREUM'S USES range from basic payment systems, asset acquisition, financing, to the digitization of everyday life, account management and market prediction, aspiring to much more in the near-term future.

IT IS VERY likely that many people often wonder what Ethereum is used for or what it is used for. Even for connoisseurs in the field there are often surprises when they learn of frequent or new utilities that they simply did not know about.

Below, we will highlight just a few of the main uses that the community has given and keeps active on the Ethereum platform.

1. **ICO (Initial Coin Offer) & DAICO (Decentralized Autonomous Organization + ICO)**

THE OPERATIONAL DYNAMICS of ICOs (financing instrument) from Ethereum is much simpler, as is the sale of tokens. Its formats and features imbue it with transparency and efficiency. Vitálik Buterin suggested merging ICOs and DAOs to create the hybrid DAICO model.

. . .

ON ONE OCCASION, a DAICO was launched with a variable called TAP (units: wei/sec, initialized to zero), somewhat different from the old ICO contract, but which also starts as a contribution, only that it is configured to determine how many Ether developers can withdraw per second, where the limit is determined by the contributors themselves. Finally, in this process, developers are given some control to avoid making a total withdrawal of the amount and to be able to leave in seconds.

1. Contract banking and financial services

FROM A MERCANTILE POINT OF VIEW, the contract services of the Ethereum Blockchain, offer a range of possibilities to be set up. In this way, they can be linked to well-known national bonds, payments, settlements, mortgages, credits and trusts among other elements.

An illustrative demonstration of this use could be represented in the hypothetical case of a person who has defaulted on his scheduled payment commitment on a loan without notifying the bank. It could be that, instead of proceeding with a bond, a long-standing Smart Contract would be codified in which the conditions and rules would be imposed.

Another avenue would be in government bonds nearing maturity that have been supported with a smart contract, where payments would be processed immediately upon maturity to the person or entity holding them.

1. Predictive markets.

ETHEREUM ALSO BENEFITS PREDICTIVE MARKETS. Although in practice there are few platforms dedicated to this productive sector of crypto from the Blockchain. The main cases of prediction markets favored by Ethereum to highlight are Gnosis (GNO) and Augur (REP).

Prediction markets are understood as certain sectors in which it is valid to consider knowing something in the future or to come up with certain results. For example, electoral processes, sporting events or auction results, among others.

In this type of scenarios, participants are motivated to predict some outcome and in case of being right, they will be benefited and rewarded with smart contracts in the Ethereum Blockchain.

FINALLY, these predictions could be used without complications in betting or to make decisions in a company when promoting a new product, which is why the process in its general context, would be very economical and rewarding.

1. **Trusts**

WHEN IN A CERTAIN situation the need for a special escrow service and an intermediary is required, Ethereum Smart Contracts are the appropriate choice, as they can currently be replaced. Only one condition would be in charge of the smart contract in a context as described, and that is to program the contract with all considerations and possible scenarios. In this way, they can be safely applied.

A GOOD EXAMPLE of this use can be represented with an escrow service in a P2P Exchange (Peer-To-Peer Network), when using smart contracts in a real estate organization as with inheritances and wills.

1. **Digital identity management**

THE MANAGEMENT of digital identities is being talked about more and more every day, and it turns out to be a key for the future of society. Based on smart contracts, it would be feasible to provide appropriate solutions and save millions of dollars in cases of information theft or monopoly.

A CLEAR EXAMPLE can be seen in the uPort projects, which offers a brilliant alternative of sovereign identity to its users, where if there is the possibility of traveling outside the country of residence, it is possible to obtain a passport through uPort. Then, when crossing the checkpoints, all the details required by the airport would be displayed in order to embark on the trip.

FINALLY, there would be no way to see or copy the digital identity data, unless the owner authenticates through the uPort application by means of his cell phone to transfer the information to the Ethereum Blockchain, which represents a trusted source of information for those who request it.

Buying, selling and trading Ethereum (Binance, Coinbase, Cex.io)

THE DIGITAL FINANCIAL market is comprehensive and is characterized by providing a wide variety of operational resources that keeps the network in constant movement second by second, its dynamics is totally active and unstoppable. Those who are part of the cryptoactive spectrum will find themselves in an environment of intense action, given the need to buy, sell and trade with a view to generating wealth and opening up a secure, trustworthy and wide-ranging exchange future.

· · ·

THERE IS a big difference between buying, selling and trading cryptocurrencies within an exchange trading system from a given virtual platform or exchange. These trading activities are carried out with the firm purpose of earning profits by making deals in the cryptocurrency market between users and subscribers with common intentions.

The buying, selling and trading of cryptocurrencies is carried out within a marketplace for such purposes. The trader will have to open an account in the corresponding platform in which he will fill out an online form. Most of these platforms within the market have an order book where you can see what users are bidding and asking for and from where they are doing it.

CRYPTOCURRENCY EXCHANGES generally accept deposits and make withdrawals in two forms. A small number of exchanges, located mainly in the United Kingdom and the United States, accept deposits in fiat currency (by fiat and unbacked) and cryptocurrencies. On the other hand, the vast majority of exchanges worldwide accept crypto-based transaction procedures, due to the regulations imposed by financial institutions on these markets for handling bank accounts.

In the event that the exchange of withdrawals and deposits is only accepted by means of cryptocurrencies, the trader must create an independent wallet that serves as a bridge between the two organizations and allows the use of the virtual currency in question to make deposits. The most common and widely used cryptocurrencies for these operations are Bitcoin, Litecoin and Ethereum.

IN ORDER TO carry out fund operations, you will need to have or buy Ethereum, in our particular case, or any other currency allowed for these transactions independently and transfer it to your wallet. Then these funds will be transferred from this wallet to the one provided by the platform to close the exchange. In this procedure you must be very sure to have the exact and precise data of the recipient or receiver, since, once the transaction is completed, it will not be possible to reverse it.

BINANCE

FOUNDED MAINLY in 2005 in Shanghai, as a Fusion System, Binance is currently one of the exchange platforms with the largest number of participants and proven trading volume in the world. Binance, as an exchange platform for cryptocurrencies, offers an operating system compatible with more than 100 digital assets today.

Binance is not regulated by any federal entity globally. A curious and interesting detail is that it is not known exactly in which country or from which precise location its operational center is located. MFSA, Malta's Financial Services Authority, issued an announcement on February 21, 2020 in which it stated that Binance "is not authorized by MFSA to work in the cryptocurrency sphere, so it is not intended for regulatory oversight by this Authority".

IF YOU HAVE funds in cryptocurrencies and want to buy, sell or trade them using Ether ETH, the native currency of Ethereum through Binance, to get a return on your digital money; the first thing you should do is to create your own account on this Exchange. Once you have created your access profile, you will have the option to trade from this important platform by following the steps below.

TO MAKE PURCHASES, for example, and already on the Binance website, the user must go to the "Markets" segment and take into account which will be his pair for negotiation within the multiple currencies available. Selecting the "Zones" tab will display a menu where the "All" button appears, which will present the group of coins to buy, with Ethereum's Ether appearing in its second place of honor after Bitcoin.

Next, click on the "Trade" to display a new tab that will generate a chart of Ethereum with the USDT value, that is; with Ether which is the cryptocurrency that follows the value of the dollar in the market. In the "Search" button you type ETH and choose the cryptocurrency with which you want to exchange the purchase, bearing in mind that Ether is available to be traded with an extensively wide number of currencies.

THIS WILL INITIATE an order to the market, generate the negotiation when you click on the buy button.

AS IN THIS EXAMPLE, we want to buy Ether with the respective pair (dollars or euros), we continue with the process by going directly to the "Place order" section, then "Purchases" and then "Market", the market price will appear and we place the desired amount to buy to easily and simply obtain the desired amount which will appear immediately in the client's wallet.

It is important to get acquainted with this very well designed and programmed digital platform, to know the steps to follow and from it, to have a tool that allows its community to perform a variety of operations with full security and protection.

BINANCE OFFERS a guarantee service with absolute support that protects its users from possible scams and fraudulent businesses. If in a negotiation one of the parties suggests to operate outside the Binance P2P platform, Binance ignores the process and immediately opens an appeal, and if the agreement is made outside the exchange; there will be no form or way of protection.

. . .

Cex.io

WITH AN OPENING REGISTRATION made in 2013 in the city of London (UK) as its date and place of foundation, to date and after almost eight years of activity;

Cex.io has become one of the most experienced exchanges in the virtual market, qualifying as one of the safest exchanges in which no customer has ever lost funds, something few players can boast about.

CEX.IO, with more than 3 million users, all active, is a platform that offers buy, sell, trade and wallet services in practically all continents.

ONE OF THE first digital platforms to emphasize cryptocurrency transactions in fiat currency pairs in dollars, euros, pounds or rubles was Cex.io. At the beginning, many international operators found themselves up against a wall, since a large number of exchanges demanded their deposits in cryptocurrencies, but Cex.io, as well as Kraken, made a remarkable change to the panorama.

To trade from Cex.io the first thing to do is to create an access account easily and free of charge in just seconds from their website, by clicking on the "Register" button to enter an email address on the page that will be displayed, then create a password and indicate your country of residence.

Attention! There are several countries in which Cex.io does not support registrations and therefore its platform does not apply. These are listed below:

Afghanistan, Bosnia, Burundi, Central African Republic, Cuba, Ethiopia, Guam, Guinea Bissau, Guyana, Iran, Iraq, Japan, Laos, Lebanon, Libya, North Korea, Mali, Pakistan, Puerto Rico, Republic of Congo, Somalia, Sri Lanka, Sudan, South Sudan, Syria, South Sudan, Trinidad and Tobago, Tunisia, Uganda, Vanuatu, Venezuela, Yemen and Zimbabwe.

Many users prefer to trade from Cex.io because they know that Ethereum is currently ranked among the most popular, recognized and used major cryptocurrencies worldwide. Ether ETH, is an attractive cryptocurrency that arouses great interest for those people who wish and seek to buy, sell, trade and exchange with Ethereum and its preferred peers in order to introduce it to the Blockchain.

Ether ETH/Ethereum is quite uniquely appropriate and enjoys special interest from those professional and expert traders who consider its price to be the most appropriate for high volume trading and exchange transactions. That is why Ethereum is said to be the best alternative for those who conceive it as the best utility asset, as well as for those who simply and solely wish to trade.

Relative to Bitcoin's price and utility value, Ethereum turns out to be much more attractive. Although it is clearly established that Ether is several times cheaper than Bitcoin, this can easily attract the attention of the public interested in obtaining a certain amount of cryptocurrencies, without being restricted to a particular currency.

THERE ARE many who choose Ether to invest or negotiate in future projects, due to the great confidence generated by its Blockchain technology inspired by the idea of decentralization of money. For this reason, Ether is one of the most traded currencies by users on the network and a common alternative for cryptographic exchanges.

For example, there are many exchanges that postulate their proposals to carry out Ether-to-dollar transactions.

Cex.io is among the leading trend-setting platforms, offering highly competitive exchange rates and terms to its more than 3 million users worldwide.

. . .

CONSIDERING the very nature of exchange services on behalf of Ethereum, the Cex.io platform provides a suitable structure with professional traders as well as beginners in mind.

THE MARKET RATES for buying and selling, etc. are transparent and clear, so that at all times participants can trust and be confident that all trades will be executed under the expected conditions. In addition, with Stop-Loss orders available on the platform, all trades will be stopped in case their price reaches levels where the transaction is irreversibly at an imminent loss. Thus, having a price change in Ethereum securities, it will be possible to minimize possible losses, as the software is programmed to provide a service according to the agreed or the most favorable conditions.

Trading transactions and other operations with cryptocurrencies are simple, fast and easy on this platform, for this we detail an example of the process that otherwise includes similar steps of start and registration similar to other exchanges:

- REGISTER on the website to get your own trading account and access buy, sell and trade page.

- SPECIFY the digital asset you wish to trade.

- SELECT THE CURRENCY in which the trade will be made and click on "Buy".

- IF USING a credit card for the purchase, the credit card must be linked.

. . .

- CHECK that all the information is correct and click on "Buy Now".

CEX.IO APPLIES a series of commissions and fees for certain and specific transactions. One of the cases is when for example deposits are made with fiat currency (not backed by commodities such as gold and silver) with Visa, here the fee for such activity ranges between 1.49% and 2.99%, very similar to deposits with MasterCard, for deposits via SWIFT, SEPA and Faster Payments no fee or activity fee is charged.

COINBASE

IT IS a virtual platform that works on the one hand as a digital wallet, which means that you can store your electronic money in a single place. In this sense, you can consider Coinbase as an application such as your trusted bank, from where you can see the amount of cryptocurrencies you own and the evolution of its value.

Similarly, fulfilling its strict function as a virtual wallet, you will have a unique email address through which other users will send you cryptocurrencies and you will have the option to make payments and trade without requiring the assistance of outsourced services.

Coinbase also offers the service of buying and selling cryptocurrencies. This means that you have the alternative to register and associate your credit card to the system and thus use your traditional money or fiat money to buy different types of cryptocurrencies, and then when you see fit you can sell and renegotiate according to your intentions.

WITH COINBASE you have a tool whose operation keeps some similarity or resemblance to others such as the application of your bank or PayPal, for example, when making a payment and receive cryptocurrencies, you can also manage it as if it were a stock market App, only instead of speculating within the stock market you can do it with the cryptocurrency market.

It is convenient that the user should be very cautious with the value of cryptocurrencies, as this is quite volatile and should evaluate how much money would be willing to put at stake or risk when deciding to make a transaction.

THE USER MUST KEEP in mind that Coinbase will charge a fee or commission every time cryptocurrencies are bought or sold. For the purchase of cryptocurrencies the commission is 1.49%, for the sale of cryptocurrencies and to exchange them for real or fiat money, the commission is 1.00%; while, for operations and transactions of assets to other wallets or virtual wallets, no fees or commissions apply. These are very general aspects configured in practically all the platforms dedicated to these commercial purposes.

It is easy to start a business protocol for buying, selling or trading on the Coinbase platform. As we have already seen and like the previous ones, the first step to be taken by the interested party is to enter the Coinbase website and make your registration in the "Register" button, which you will find in the top right of the page where once the new window opens, you will have to enter the required personal data and follow the steps that in a simple and friendly way will be requested to complete the entire process in order to have a Coinbase account.

You must be very careful to enter real data and personal information without errors or omissions. Once all the requirements are fulfilled and uploaded, the user will be able to make the operations of their choice.

. . .

TO BUY, sell and trade cryptocurrencies from this system, click on the "Buy/Sell" button that appears on the upper left side of the screen, then a new window will appear from which the cryptocurrency trading is performed.

Once there, you must first choose the digital currency you want to buy and then in the pair box the amount in fiat money you want to buy. On the right side of the screen there is a breakdown of the amounts that are being handled and the value of the commissions, and finally you have to click on the "Buy Ethereum" button.

FROM THERE, the buyer will be redirected to a new screen where he/she will click on the "Confirm Purchase" button to successfully close the transaction. Once the whole process has been completed, it is likely that a verification message will be received via SMS for the code with which the transaction will be confirmed and completed. The transaction will be processed instantly if you have used a credit card, if you have used a bank account, it will take between 24 and 48 hours.

WE HAVE SEEN THAT BUYING, selling and trading Ethereum through Binance, Cex.io and Coinbase exchanges among many others is similar in many aspects. It is a similar process between them with somewhat similar characteristics, especially in the registration phase. The difference lies in the benefits, facilities and extensions that these exchanges offer to the market, hence the position they have in the commercial ranking:

THE COINMARKETCAP PLATFORM RANKS, groups and evaluates in its performance the main cryptocurrency Spot Exchanges in the world, currently 310; based on traffic, trading volume, liquidity and confidence in the legitimacy of their reported trading volumes. CoinMarketCap ranks the houses we have broken down, as follows:

- IN THE NUMBER 1 POSITION: Binance, with a score of 9.8
  - In the number 2 position: CoinBase, with a score of 8.8.

- ON POSITION NUMBER 53: Cex.io, with a score of 4.7

CRYPTOCURRENCY EXCHANGES ARE platforms that allow and give users and traders the opportunity to buy and sell cryptocurrencies, derivatives and other cryptocurrency-related assets.

Nowadays, there is a wide range and variety of cryptocurrency exchanges to choose from, being able to select the one that best meets the expectations of the interested party, and all of them have great advantages in one aspect or another. It is recommended to learn more about the best cryptocurrency exchanges and thus select the one that best helps and meets the investment objectives related to the crypto spectrum.

To culminate this interesting section, let's globalize a bit with respect to what Tradear means, an activity that is closely and totally linked to this commercial and financial dynamics on the network.

TRADER IS DEFINED as any individual who performs the function of investor or speculator who carries out his activity in the financial markets with the sole purpose of generating or producing profits for himself in the short, medium or long term.

A trader can perform his work independently or dedicate himself to the financial activity of a banking entity as a Market Maker in the Front Office trading desks or in a treasury.

. . .

ANY TYPE of product or investment modality can constitute the operative spectrum of a trader, this can be spot or futures; investment products, fixed income, commodities, interest rates, currencies, crypto-assets, etc. His availability and experience will be influential in his exposure to different asset classes that make up the financial market, as each market has its own characteristics.

ON THE BASIS of his purchasing power, each trader will be able to define his own rules, norms and behavioral guidelines and thus carry out his stock market study, evaluating what will be his most appropriate and optimal risk-benefit ratio. Besides, it is convenient to know that an investor becomes a trader based on work, experience, conduct (a very important condition) and an appropriate monetary management.

The investor agent or trader will make his own investment decisions, taking into account the technical and fundamental analysis, or he will be able to make decisions through his automatic investment systems that execute themselves, created from programmed price rules that invest in most cases, in very short periods of time. This trading modality is special and is known as High Frequency Trading (HFT).

Cryptocurrency trading, however, involves investing around the movements of its prices through a trading account, making negotiations of buying and selling of underlying cryptocurrencies in a trading market.

Cryptocurrency trading is oriented in taking a financial position in routing towards the value of a cryptocurrency against the dollar, in dollar/cryptocurrency pair or crypto against crypto, through pairs. Contracts for Difference (CFDs), are a very notorious way to trade cryptocurrencies, as they allow a greater range of flexibility, the use of leverage and the ability to fix buy or sell positions, in other words; short or long.

If the investor or trader assumes that the price of the cryptocurrency is going to fall, he would take a sell position or go short. Now, if the investor considers that the value will be increasing, he would take a buy position or go long. This procedure could be very advantageous considering the fact that the cryptocurrency market is prone to very aggressive price movements. It is important to take into account that volatility increases risk. In addition to a virtual currency, there are many risks that may well negatively affect the future of a trade.

HOW TO STORE **Ethereum (Talk about Binance, Trezor Wallet and Ledger Nano).**

WE HAVE BEEN TOLD since we were children that "To run, we must first walk". Wise words! Well, we can apply a perfect analogy in this case to how to store cryptocurrencies.

THE FIRST THING we will need before being able to receive an Ether, is to have a place to store it; for this it is imperative to have a wallet or wallet, as it is called in cryptographic jargon. It is basically a software resource that will allow us to store our virtual funds, perform operations and other transactions in a very simple way, as well as review and monitor the available balance.

It should be noted that the operation of Ethereum wallets does not correspond to the use of typical conventional physical wallets. In fact, Ether as such will not be stored in a wallet as such, in a bank account or somewhere else.

Ether, just like any other known virtual currency in the world, does not exist in any physical or tangible form. The only thing that exists in the cryptographic spectrum, are only records in the Blockchain and the wallet created can only interact with the Blockchain that allows it to enable transactions or operations that you want to perform exclusively within the same network.

The wallets have their own public addresses, consisting of case-sensitive strings of letters and numbers. In case there is a person who wants to send Ether, he/she will send it to an address, which is also known as "public key", a resource that is basically in charge of transferring the ownership of cryptocurrencies from one point to another.

A "PRIVATE KEY" is what is actually stored in our virtual wallet together with a password that will be necessary to close transactions and also to unlock the coins available and that we have within the network. As with any operation or resource of a virtual private personal nature, any key must be kept jealously guarded secret in order to avoid unauthorized invasion and possible embezzlement of the funds in Ether.

Both public and private access keys are paired, which means that in order to make a transaction, both strings of letters and numbers must necessarily match.

THE EASIEST WAY TO store the Ether you have is to take a third-party wallet and store it there. Clarifying this scenario, for example; taking a wallet that has been provided by an exchange. This way, you will have much easier access to the funds, and if you keep the tokens in that exchange, this will be of great help to carry out any kind of operation in a faster way.

HOWEVER, if you opt for this methodology, it is important to be clear and understand that you will be giving total control of the funds to the exchange and that is just by giving the possibility to a third party to store the private keys. But be careful, the recent history of cryptocurrencies is saturated and full of confirmed cases of fraudulent exchanges and theft in which users have lost everything.

The Ethereum platform allows its visitors to create their own personal wallet for private use, being able to choose from a variety of options, so that only the owner will have full control over his private key and by default, everything inherent to the access and status of his digital funds on the network.

In the Ethereum platform there are two types or categories of wallets: hot and cold. Let's define.

- HOT WALLET: It is one that stores private keys online and enjoy very easy access from virtually any device and place in the world, it will only be necessary to have internet connection. This is not the best option, as they are very vulnerable and sensitive to any invasive attack, which can lead to funds being stolen.

- COLD WALLET: This is a wallet that stores private keys offline and can only be connected to the internet when the owner pairs the wallet to a connection.

THERE IS no doubt that the latter is the most secure and very unlikely to be a victim of hacker attacks or cybercrime.

About storing Ethereum, we began by saying a popular expression, remember? Well, first things first, and that is to create your own wallet, something that turns out to be relatively quite easy, practical and simple, even more so when it is especially the platform of the system itself that provides us with the service. This is MyEtherWallet, the official wallet provided by Ethereum.

Now let's see how to set it up. First of all, we must enter the website of the crypto in question paying due and careful attention to the security reminders that will appear on the screen and will be welcoming us.

It is suggested to take the necessary time to read and analyze them, as they are very useful to reach a proper and better understanding of the process that we are about to continue, knowing how the procedure works, learning everything we should do and what we should avoid, only in this way it will be possible to give due protection to our funds.

AFTER READING THE CONDITIONS, tips and suggestions, we will find the option that will allow us to create our password and start the configuration of the new wallet. Once a sufficiently secure password has been created, the next step is to download the file from which the private keys for the wallet are accumulated. As all key records and the possibility of being intercepted even from unknown intruders, it is always advisable to store this file in a safe and secret place.

Next comes a very significant and very important step, saving the private key of our wallet. It is advisable to make a backup copy, memorize it, write it down on a piece of paper and keep it in a safe place that is difficult to access. We must be careful to do everything necessary to ensure that the key will be properly safeguarded and that no one will be able to access it. Remember that we are talking about managing cryptocurrency funds and we must prevent third parties from accessing them.

We have successfully created and configured our new wallet from the platform provided directly by Ethereum in its MyEther-Wallet portal. Now and the next time we want to log in to our wallet, all we have to do is authorize ourselves on the web site using our access keys. From there we will have the opportunity to see the public address of our wallet already enabled to receive Ether, as well as the balance, movements and verifiable records in it.

THE ORIENTATION GUIDE we have developed is focused on the configuration of the easiest and probably the most used Ether wallet in the market and the virtual industry dedicated to crypto. There are many and varied amounts of wallets on the network, which count and offer a wide range of options. Although there is a common principle in all of them; the installation and configuration processes are somewhat particular in each of the cases.

STORE WITH BINANCE

RECENTLY, on April 27, 2021 Binance launched to the digital market a new virtual wallet as an alternative to use and store cryptocurrencies without any difficulty, in a simple and friendly format. A way to bring its users a little further ahead in the pursuit of their goals towards the freedom of money.

BINANCE CHAIN IS a native Binance mobile wallet, which provides a secure and convenient space to easily store funds outside of the Binance platform with multiple features that will ensure a unique experience with online trading.

The use of Binance Chain is free, by downloading the App and without any costs for its availability on your device. At the same time and as products related to the Blockchain product range, no commissions will be paid and there are no hidden ones. The way to pay commissions is given only for network and other common transactions, however, Binance does its best to minimize operating expenses.

WITH THE BINANCE Chain browser-based trading extension, it will be possible to perform secure, immediate and reliable funds transfer. Between Ethereum and other peers, the cross-chain transfer function applies to Binance-owned blockchains.

· · ·

FROM THE BINANCE CHAIN ITSELF, the extension can also be used among other products within the platform to authenticate transactions without the need to provide a private key or login. These will be securely archived in its storage location and together with a password will be encrypted.

FOR THIS UNIFICATION TO take effect, the extension requires incorporating connection codes with the browser's "open web application in tab" in conjunction with the extension set simultaneously. The extension will request permission to access any web page.

IT IS ALWAYS important to keep all keys and passwords, as well as devices external to the web platform, in safe and reliable places, away from possible insecure entities or in conditions susceptible to theft or loss. Digital funds need to be protected at all times and places. An attack by a hacker is possible, and if it happens, the funds will be lost.

STORAGE WITH TREZOR **Wallet**

THIS IS one of the leading cryptocurrency wallets developed in cold or Cold Storage. Satoshi Labs, founded in 2013 by Marek "Slush" Palatinus and Pavol "Stick" Rusnak in the Czech Republic, is behind Trezor Wallet, a leading cryptocurrency storage device. It is currently headquartered in Prague, Czech Republic; the place of its founding, with human capital of over 50 workers on its official payroll.

Just like any other hardware wallet, Trezor Wallet offers its public and users a higher security system than a software wallet, since their personal passwords are archived or stored in a physical device and the funds of its subscribers are never in direct contact with the Internet, making it practically impossible for them to be stolen, much less hacked.

THE TREZOR WALLET system supports a very large number of coins and ERC20 tokens, more than 1000, which gives you the alternative of having all your assets together and in one place.

Currently there are two types or versions of its virtual appliance available: Trezor One and Trezor Model. Very distant from their value or market price, the main differences are centered on the amount of cryptocurrencies that each of them, the screen format, the selection of buttons in its menu and the possibility of making "Shamir BackUp" (backup).

Trezor Wallet is one of the first to go on sale in the digital market, is the one that has sold more units and has the largest number of active users around, counting to its credit a little more than one million subscribers in the world.

MOST OF THE FORUMS, opinions and comments issued about Trezor Wallet by its diverse communities are very positive; highlighting above all the security of the product, its quality of construction and how simple the configuration process is for its first use.

Complaints are also received, as it is obviously a product for human consumption through the virtual network. The most common is the request and obligation to connect the wallet directly to the computer to process transactions with cryptocurrencies, although this novelty is present in all devices designed for this purpose.

Storing with Ledger Nano It is Ledger Nano one of the leading producers of hardware wallets in the world. Hardware wallets (HW), represent most probably the most secure, robust and strongest way, form and modality you can have to store cryptocurrencies such as Ethereum, Bitcoin, NEO or any other coin.

· · ·

THE WAY HARDWARE wallets reach their maximum security is by storing your private key, far out of reach of hackers or other cyber-criminals seeking to appropriate your virtual funds.

THE PRIVATE KEY configuration is mathematically closely related to all crypto addresses and the public keys generated by it. This key will be responsible for "stamping" the signature of all offline transactions so that there are no intruders attempting to attack and violate the privacy of your remote wallet.

Most of the existing inventory of hardware wallets usually also use a second screen or device to corroborate the wallet's actions and sign the transaction. So, if a hacker manages to gain control over your processor, he will not be able to do any damage, as he will also need access to the physical device that connects to the client's computer.

LEDGER NANO IS a hardware wallet storage device that works normally like any other similar device. It must be connected to a computer, the PIN is chosen and a recovery phrase of 24 is received that will add a layer of security to the wallet.

WHAT IS **gas and why is it so important for transactions?**

GAS IS a specific unit of measurement used by Ethereum to quantify the work produced by its platform, in the execution of transactions or any type of interaction generated on the network. Gas is one of the most used and most seen terms within the Ethereum ecosystem, a word that even users see frequently in their transactions or within the interaction of their Smart Contracts, even wondering what it is.

. . .

GAS IS NOT JUST a unit of measurement, it is essential for every-thing that happens, happens and happens within the Ethereum plat-form, the impact on its ecosystem is broad and immense. Let's see in a practical and simple way, through a dynamic example; the impor-tance of this term and its development in the Ethereum Blockchain itself.

YOU WANT to buy a new computer, and for that you need to travel by cab. Knowing that it will take you 30 minutes to get to the tech-nology store and for every minute the taxi meter of the High Service company recharges a value of $0.50, you have the option of using the services of its competition that does it for $0.40 you will then require between $12 or $15 to get to your destination.

A similar situation occurs in Ethereum. Each process or activity step in Ethereum represents a specific and unvarying cost that stipu-lates it gas, which is the same as in the case of the taxi meter per minute driven.

Clearly, operations in Ethereum are made up of much smaller functions, each with a point value of gas or estimated travel time, of which the sum total will tell us the final overall value of gas for that operation, which is equal to the total time going to the tech store leaving from home. Now, within Ethereum, how much is the grand total to pay for gas to carry out the operation in question?

In our analogy the transfer represents a variant cost of $12 to $15, being able to select which company to travel with in order to save as much as possible. Something quite similar happens in Ethereum, gas has a stipulated price in Ether that is created according to the supply and demand of operations within the Ethereum platform.

. . .

THIS MEANS that the price of gas in Ether will always be variable, considering that in this case the user can choose the value he will pay for that gas, and if there is a miner in the network who is happy with the offer, he will process the transaction and execute it. Thus, we can understand that the concept and function of gas within the Ethereum platform are of relevant utility and importance.

Blockchains or Blockchains using Proof Of Work (PoW) protocols all tend to operate under the same condition. A fee must always be paid for a transaction to be carried out, then it will be accepted and uploaded to a Blockchain, for a cost benefit in favor of the miners who will take it and include it in a block.

Once included in that block, the transaction will be confirmed and validated by the network, then the orders found in the transactions will be executed and finally accepted. This is a simple and valid way to see the PoW, which means that in order to have access to a Blockchain network, a small fee is always required. Usually these payments are made in decimal units of the operating currency on the Blockchain.

SUCH IS the case of Bitcoin, in which each transaction is paid in satoshis, the smallest decimal unit of this cryptocurrency. Here is its objective:

- TO ESTABLISH a cost to every transaction executed on the network. Thus maintaining the network's functionality incentives, a task proper to the miners.

- TO PRESERVE and guarantee the security of the system, avoiding indiscriminate access to resources. Because of its high costs, a hacker would not engage in spamming or DoS (cyber attack whose purpose is to disable a computer system for a certain time by saturating access to it with numerous illegitimate requests), towards the network, as it would be excessively costly.

THE ABOVE APPLIES to Bitcoin and is equally valid for Ethereum, with the only difference being that the creators of Ethereum sought a different approach to solving this problem. The determination to create the gas mechanism is due to the fact that Ethereum itself is not a cryptocurrency, but a broad platform that works as a whole in a way analogous to a computer, known as a Blockchain Computer.

EACH TRANSACTION in Ethereum is a small program, which gives instructions to the Ethereum Virtual Machine (EVM), so that this machine then translates them as an action or series of them to be performed. It is in this plane where Ethereum and its Ethereum Virtual Machine (EVM) turn out to be similar in operation to Bitcoin and its Bitcoin Script. The caveat for Ethereum, however, is that it is actually much more flexible.

A DETAIL of relevance is that in Ethereum, its developers determined to credit an invariable value to the different and multiple transactions that can be carried out on its platform. Thus, each transaction has a cost and a specific and determined gas value that will not suffer variations, regardless of the fluctuation in the price of Ether, its native currency.

THE CONSTANT AND invariable value of gas is based on the fact that, although the price of Ether is certainly volatile, the computational costs of the operations remain stable. For such a reason, the staff of Ethereum developers, can differentiate, with the creation of gas; between the computational cost and true value of operations at a given time. Such is the functionality of this system that allows Ethereum and its network to remain constantly operational, without being affected by the rise or fall of Ether.

LET'S see the case in which a Smart Contract has the function of "Consult Balance Of An Address", this activity in the network could have the value of 1000 Gas, that will always be its value. This means that the realization of this operation in Ethereum, always has to be paid a very small commission in Ether, inherent to the amount of gas used to achieve the realization of such action in the Blockchain.

All of the above, makes us highlight three vital and important aspects within the Ethereum platform:

GAS UNIT:

The gas unit is represented by the amount of gas possible to be attributed to a particular instruction, although without monetary value.

2.GAS PRICE:

IT IS the commission payment given for each unit of gas. It is a price chosen to be paid for each unit and is made using the decimals of Ether, Gwei. This commission is the one that will allow the user to enjoy priority and more attention. By paying more for each unit of gas used, the faster the miners will take the transaction in question and move it to a block.

GAS LIMIT:

.   .   .

IT IS the representative value that determines the maximum amount of gas units that the Ethereum network is in a position to trade in a given space of time. It is the maximum limit, which miners will not be able to exceed or exceed at any time.

IT IS clear here that this is a somewhat more complex process compared to what happens in the case of Bitcoin and other cryptocurrencies derived from it. The reason is based on the fact that in Ethereum, the Ethereum Virtual Machine (EVM) is conditioned to handle a specific amount of information. In such a way that, in order to work with this information limit, this work measurement has been designed and created, so that the level of computational work that the network can perform at the same time can be controlled.

IT IS convenient to know how much is the limit or Gas Limit. This will depend on whether we are referring to a transaction or operation with a block or Smart Contract. 1,21,000 units of gas is the Gas Limit of a transaction. This means that there will be no single transaction or operation in Ethereum that consumes a higher value and is located above 21,000 units of gas.

2.THE GAS LIMIT **of a Smart Contract is higher and variable.**

The reason for this to occur is based on the fact that Smart Contracts are susceptible to have a certain and determined complexity in their interactions, which implies and lies in a higher gas level. This Gas Limit tends to be between 130,000 and 145,000 gas units.

.   .   .

3.8 MILLION UNITS OF GAS, the maximum value established for the Gas Limit of a block. This means that miners are free to include as many transactions and interactions through Smart Contracts as possible, taking into account that they cannot exceed the limit of 8 million units of gas.

IN REFERENCE to this third point and its maximum or limit level, it is very relevant, since it provides the possibility of taking action against the "Halting Problem", a computational problem that allows us to be aware of whether a computer program is executed in an infinite loop, with only the input and programming data.

Faced with this situation, it would trace a delicate problem for the Blockchain that could result in a denial of services (DoS). However, thanks to the fact that Ethereum sets a precise Gas Limit for each block, there will not be any operation on this platform that will be able to exceed the pre-designed limit.

TWO

ETHEREUM, ETHEREUM CLASSIC OR BITCOIN?

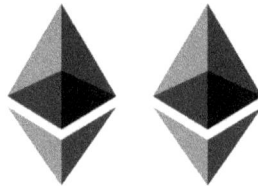

The existence in the market of a product, good or service is subject to changes; changes or modifications ranging from the design, image, structure or even its own name. The planning and development of a new creation has from its conception an idea and a purpose, the intention to fulfill certain objectives and satisfy the needs to which such creation is directed.

WITHIN THE CRYPTOGALAXY, the menu of options, brands and sub-brands that unfolds is gigantic; the more than 7,000 existing digital currencies and the infinity of products, systems, programs and services that we can find in it is so wide, that it would take us days, months and years of research to specialize in a single item, which will probably produce modifications and more changes in the development of our project. It is a back-and-forth of novelties, we understand that not everything will remain inert once it sees the light of day.

NEXT, let's get to know some of the marked differences that exist between three participating elements and members of this gigantic encrypted galaxy: Ethereum, Ethereum Classic and Bitcoin, the largest and most impactful projects within the Blockchain community in the world and thus understand how the process and dynamics that have imbued it with the value and importance it enjoys today have been.

Ethereum Classic, let's see them as two different cryptocurrencies that share a common origin and some of the aspects related to the reason for their diversification.

ETHEREUM AND ETHEREUM Classic were two exactly identical virtual currencies until the creation and closure of the 1,920,000 block, right up to the moment that the Fork took place, a change in the currency's protocol that was intended to retake the tokens lost after the hacking done to the DAO (Decentralized Autonomous Organization).

This measure was taken with the intention of providing a solution that the majority of the Ethereum community adopted with the purpose of recovering and returning to their rightful owners the lost Ether, 1 Ether for every 100 DAOs, along with a Smart Contract of a complex nature. As a result of this event and as a result of the solution, instead of one of the coins disappearing as it was initially believed, now both continue to trade on the Blockchain.

. . .

AMONG THE MOST notorious differences we can find between Ethereum (ETH) and Ethereum Classic (ETC), we have that:

(*) By May 10, 2021.

ETHEREUM CLASSIC

ETH BORN in 2015 ETH emerges as a native currency Very high level developer system.
   It is moving to Proof of Stake with the upcoming

NO DEFINED issuance cap
   High impact e-marketing support

BACKED by major influencers and personalities

NUMBER 2 POSITION in top cryptocurrencies

HIGH VALUE in its price Capitalization of 41,801,443,830.00 $ Best updates on the network

ETHEREUM ETC WAS BORN in 2016 ETC arises as a result of a possible hacking

GROWING system of developers

. . .

IT HAS a Proof of Work consensus algorithm.

Will have an issuance cap of between 210 million and 230 million

E-MARKETING SUPPORT INITIATED
Backing from lesser-known figures

RANKED 16TH in the top cryptocurrencies* Low value relative to ETH

MARKET CAPITALIZATION of $600,788,003.00

LOWER UPDATES than ETH

THESE WOULD COME to be the most outstanding differences at the moment, since in essence they are the product of the same platform with the same principle, only that as an emergency measure action had to be taken in the face of the scandalous embezzlement occurred on June 17, 2016 for an amount of $56,196,000.00 $ USD, represented approximately by 3,600,000.00 ETH at a value of 15.61 the unit.

CONSIDERING the premise that both coins could be considered "sisters" and on the basis of their own differences in form and action, we will proceed next to see in the same reference, what would consequently be the main differences between the largest cryptocurrencies on the network and occupying the first two places in the top of quotations.

MORE ABOUT ETHEREUM **Classic vs. Ethereum differences?**

ALTHOUGH ETHEREUM CLASSIC ETC has value as a speculative digital asset that investors can trade, Ethereum ETH is considered the most legitimate and the most traded.

In early 2021, the Chicago Mercantile Exchange (CME) approved the trading of Ether futures. Only Bitcoin and Ether have been approved for such transactions. Futures are derivative contracts on an underlying security with a fixed price and expiration date. Ether futures allow investors to trade Ether for speculation, but also to hedge a prominent position in ETH or perhaps other cryptocurrencies.

We can determine how the investment community to ETC versus ETH by analyzing how much capital or investment dollars they are committing to the two coins. When comparing the two market capitalizations of the two cryptocurrencies, ETH is the clear winner. The market capitalization of a cryptocurrency is calculated by multiplying the price of the coin, based on a fiat currency such as the U.S. dollar, by the coins or tokens in circulation.

ETC HAS 116.3 million coins outstanding with a market cap of $10.9 billion, while ETH has approximately 115.6 million outstanding and a market cap of over $464.12 billion. ETC trades at $93.82 while ETH trades at over $4,012.00 per coin as of May 13, 2021.

. . .

ALTHOUGH BOTH NETWORKS offer smart contracts, the potential for the aforementioned security concerns surrounding ETC will likely push investors to invest in ETH and adopt Ethereum smart contracts versus Ethereum Classic.

UNDERSTANDING ETHEREUM CLASSIC

ETHEREUM CLASSIC FACILITATES the execution of smart contracts by offering the benefit of decentralized governance. In other words, contracts can be enforced without the involvement of a third party, such as a lawyer.

Smart contracts are similar to if-then statements, meaning that, if the required actions within the contract have been fulfilled, then the parameters of the responsive contract will be completed. If the parameters of the contract have not been met, then there may be a penalty, a fee or the contract may be voided, depending on the terms stated at the beginning of the contract.

FOR EXAMPLE, in a real estate transaction, if the contract stated that a deposit was to be paid in advance by a certain date and the funds were not received, the contract could be voided. Smart contracts are contained within a distributed ledger or Blockchain network. A distributed ledger is a ledger of transactions and contracts, which are held and maintained in a decentralized manner in multiple locations.

The agreement between a buyer and seller is written in lines of code within the smart contract, which is self-executing, according to the terms of the contract. As a result, there is no need for external oversight or censorship by a central authority, as the code controls the execution of the contract.

. . .

ETHEREUM CLASSIC GOALS

SINCE THE SPLIT, there have been many updates and improvements to the Ethereum Classic project. The goal of the project remains to work towards becoming a global payment network using smart contracts that can function without centralized governance.

As with other cryptocurrencies, Ethereum Classic will likely continue to strive to be a digital store of value, meaning that it can be stored and exchanged without losing its value. The digital store of value for a cryptocurrency includes its purchasing power that can be quickly converted into cash or used to purchase another asset, similar to money.

POSSIBLE LIMITATIONS of Ethereum Classic Although both Ethereum and Ethereum Classic offer smart contracts and seek the same market, Ethereum has gained popularity as the more legitimate of the two networks. Furthermore, Ethereum's ETH is second only to Bitcoin as the world's most popular cryptocurrency.

One of the main concerns with Ethereum Classic is the potential limitations when it comes to scalability. Typically, the network can handle 15 transactions per second, but that number is much lower than payment networks like Visa, which handles over a thousand transactions per second. Although Ethereum Classic has gone through many software upgrades, the scalability of its payment systems remains one of its biggest challenges going forward.

In addition, security is likely to remain an issue with smart contracts, particularly since Ethereum Classic has already experienced a hack and theft of millions of dollars. These concerns could potentially prevent smart contracts through Ethereum Classic from being used in major financial and real estate transactions.

Cryptocurrency market regulations continue to develop, which may or may not change how Ethereum Classic and other networks operate. For example, the Securities and Exchange Commission (SEC) does not consider Ethereum or Bitcoin securities because of their decentralized networks.

Without being considered a security, some cryptos may have challenges in being approved for inclusion in various financial products that contain a basket of securities, stocks and bonds, such as exchange-traded funds and mutual funds. Going forward, uncertainty remains around the regulatory landscape for Ethereum Classic, as well as other less popular Blockchain networks.

ETHEREUM CLASSIC **and its future**

ETHEREUM CLASSIC'S future looks less bright than Ethereum, as Ethereum is considered the more legitimate of the two networks, especially with Ethereum Classic's security concerns.

Investors have lost confidence in ETC over the years due to attacks on the system, and until ETC can redevelop its code and software to prevent future attacks, Ethereum Classic may have challenges ahead. However, it remains to be seen how smart contracts will develop within the Ethereum Classic project and whether they can be adopted for widespread use.

BETWEEN BITCOIN and Ethereum we find the following differentiating aspects:

ITS CREATORS.

BITCOIN WAS CREATED by an entity identified as Satoshi Nakamoto of whom we have no location, physical traits or any personal contact. It is believed that Nakamoto could be a group of developers who under this pseudonym created Bitcoin, Blockchain technology and the concept of cryptocurrencies.

ETHEREUM WAS CREATED by a large team of developers led by the young Vitálik Buterin, a precursor and entrepreneur who had the initial vision of a grand and ambitious project, with a more complex and broader structure than Bitcoin, trying to give a twist and transformation to the world of cryptocurrencies with the staging of Turing Complete Smart Contracts.

Buterin is a globally known person, public figure and social relationist who constantly issues opinions and interviews about Ethereum and its growth.

DEVELOPMENT INVESTMENT

BITCOIN'S DEVELOPMENT was complete and totally free, without any interest or initial economic investment. So much so, that Satoshi Nakamoto developed his own software without resorting to soliciting loans or fundraising for creation support. In fact, the initial Core that participated in Bitcoin's development did so without receiving any kind of payment for its work.

THE CASE and situation prior to the founding of Ethereum is very different. Its early development was supported and sustained by an economic fundraising that managed to reach the sum of 18 million dollars through an Initial Coin Offering (ICO). This gave Ethereum the title of the first crypto ICO in the world, one of the few to emerge under this project, achieving success and growth quite clear and very well defined.

. . .

DECENTRALIZATION

THE MOST DECENTRALIZED cryptocurrency that exists world-wide is Bitcoin, besides being the network with the largest number of nodes, more global miners, developers, forks and computing power.

THE ETHEREUM PROJECT is a platform that in its beginnings saw its reputation compromised by breaking the firmness and immutability of the Blockchain, by restarting an important part of its presence in the network with the intention of recovering the funds extracted from the DAO organization after a robbery carried out to it. These actions, carried out under a series of contestable actions and brought as a consequence the division of the community and the Blockchain, generating a new cryptocurrency: ETC Ethereum Classic.

PRICE **of the asset**

IT TURNS out to be the first appreciable differentiating element at a glance between the two currencies. Bitcoin has always been at the top of the quotation, a condition that gives it character, respect, maturity and a privilege that generates from the network; trust, a larger inventory of users than other currencies and commercial presence of outstanding value.

ETHEREUM, represented by its token Ether, has a much lower price, which, although it has been growing, remains well below

Bitcoin. There are many users impacted by the worrying fact that Ethereum Smart Contracts tokens have a much higher weighting than the currency itself (Ether) that represents them on the Blockchain.

However, the common mistake we often make is to look at the price and not the capitalization.

Coin issuance At this point, Bitcoin as a cryptocurrency is destined to a finite existence, since its coin issuance has been established for a total of 21 million Bitcoins, an amount that can never be exceeded. It is to be considered that the issuance of Bitcoins every day brings it closer to its final moment as a currency, until it reaches "0", possibly in the year 2140. It is therefore a deflationary currency.

For its part Ethereum has to its credit a total inflationary issuance and infinite issuance of coins in general. This second aspect is a frequent focus of discussion in the community, with no consensus on what to do.

In addition to this, Ethereum manages an inflation control to prevent inflation from occurring and reaching levels above 2% per year, considering the total number of active coins within the network. This is feasible and possible, given that the generation of coins per block is low, representing 2 Ether every 15 seconds per mined block on average.

Crypto mining A very big feature to differentiate Bitcoin from Ethereum is the mining process. We should note first of all that Bitcoin uses the renowned Proof of Work (PoW) format, employing the HashCash algorithm and the advanced SHA-256 hash function to perform the computational work. This is a mining model that currently can only be performed with the use of ASIC miners due to the computational power load that only Bitcoin has on the network.

ANOTHER CONDITION that highlights the difference between the two currencies is that every 10 minutes a new block is completed and generated, every 2016 blocks difficulty adjustments are applied and it has a halving (halving) every 210,000 blocks every 4 years on average. To date, the coin production per mined block is 6.25 BTC.

Ethereum for its part, uses the same Proof of Work (PoW) through an algorithm named Dabber-Hashimoto (Ethash) in conjunction with the Keccak hash function, a function very similar to SHA. Ethereum mining is memory intensive, so at first it was very resistant to ASICs, an operational condition that was overcome in 2018 when the first ASIC for ETH, the now known AntMiner E3, was released. In addition to this, mining in Ethereum is still possible with the use of GPUs, something that does not apply and is not compatible with Bitcoin.

OTHER OUTSTANDING AND different operational characteristics of Ethereum is that every 10 to 20 seconds it generates a new block, its difficulty settings are executed continuously and it does not have a halving system, since its issuance value decreases according to a consensus reached in the community. Currently, the generation of cryptocurrencies for each new block mined in Ethereum is 2 Ether.

HANDLING **of commissions**

BITCOIN HAS A VERY particular and different point, with respect to Ethereum on how and on the modality of handling its mining commissions. These take into account values such as the complexity of the same according to the number of inputs and outputs, as this situation has an impact on the dimension of space used by the transaction. The price of the transaction and the respective commission to be paid are determined by the space occupied and dictated by the supply and demand generated by the users themselves, according to the fluidity of the network.

This means that, if the network is very congested, the high

demand for transactions will cause the supply of space in the blocks to be insufficient to meet everyone's needs. Otherwise, miners will give priority to those who pay the most satoshis per byte fee. If you want to be confirmed for the next block, you will have to pay a more attractive fee. Those who pay less will be considered and processed when the overhead is lower.

BELOW IS the statement that determines the amount to be paid for commissions:

TX Cost (BTC) = (TX in Bytes * Price per Byte of the network) * BTC Cost In Ethereum's commission scheme we do not talk about storage, we talk about Gas, or what is the same as saying: computational power to be consumed. Gas is a unit of measurement used in Ethereum to quantify the amount of computing power it will take to process a specific action within the Ethereum Virtual Machine (EVM). This measure of Gas has its own limitations, such is the case that a normal transaction cannot consume more than 21,000 UG (Units of Gas), in contrast Smart Contracts are, in this sense; virtually unlimited.

The units of Gas are represented by a cost that is measured in Gwei (the decimal value unit of Ether). To determine the total amount to be paid per transaction, a formula is posed between the total Gas required for the transaction, which will be equal to the cost of the unit of Gas per Gwei, multiplied by the value of the Ether. Namely:

Tx Cost (ETH) = ((Gas TX * Gas Cost) *0.000000001) * Ether Cost As can be seen, the formulation and handling of commissions in both cryptos is very different, although they all eventually reach the hands of the miners.

SMART CONTRACTS

. . .

CONSIDERED as one of the most relevant differences for its weight, robustness and enormous potential between Bitcoin and Ethereum, are the Smart Contracts. However, before we start specifying these differences; we will offer a brief concept about Smart Contracts.

A smart contract refers to a contract that executes itself without the involvement or intermediation of third parties and is "written" as is, as a computer program or software, rather than through traditional, printed, legal textual language. Computers play a very important role for Smart Contracts.

IT IS NOT JUST a matter of digitally archiving some documentation or allowing an electronic signature, as has traditionally been done, but rather these programs perform and carry out analysis by activating any part of the document, applying its internal logic.

THE CREATION of Bitcoin materialized with a very limited functionality of these contracts, and it is feasible to take advantage of their full potential thanks to the Bitcoin Script. This environment has a series of OP_CODES that are processed by the nodes and support the programming of logic in the execution of the transaction itself, functionality that gave Bitcoin the qualification of programmable money.

BITCOIN SCRIPT IS A MUCH MORE limited computer language than Ethereum, mainly because it is not Turing Complete (capacity that allows a computer to be programmed to perform any type of operation). In addition to this, it does not have its own language in an intermediate native form that facilitates development, which results in a rather complex issue for programming advanced systems.

This obvious weakness in Bitcoin was used as a great opportunity for Ethereum to gain a niche. This opened the doors and established its Ethereum Virtual Machine (EVM), a powerful virtual machine capable of executing commands with an exceptional Full Turing capability. It has a language very similar to JavaScript, this way every programmer will have the capacity and possibility to develop scripts (Smart Contracts) to push towards its Blockchain.

Thanks to all this, Ethereum obtained as a result, being the platform capable of deploying all kinds of decentralized applications, used through DApps par excellence. However, it is not free from certain limitations, and, even so; Ethereum has an outstanding advantage, so wide that it has allowed it to take advantage of it to develop an extensive ecosystem of decentralized applications focused on the financial industry (DeFi) Decentralized Finance.

A sector of the emerging network could well become the preamble to massification for cryptocurrencies.

Before all these great steps taken by Ethereum, Bitcoin has not been a mere spectator, currently has several purposes that aim to contribute to develop a Smart Contracts Turing Complete Ecocryptosystem. All this and much more with the intention of expanding the potential range of the network.

SOMETHING more about differences between Ethereum and Bitcoin Ether (ETH), the cryptocurrency of the Ethereum network, is arguably the second most popular digital token after Bitcoin (BTC). In fact, as the second largest cryptocurrency by market capitalization, comparisons between Ether and BTC are natural.

ETHER AND BITCOIN are similar in many ways: each is a digital currency that is traded through online exchanges and stored in various types of cryptocurrency wallets. Both tokens are decentralized, meaning they are neither issued nor regulated by a central bank or other authority.

Both make use of the distributed accounting technology known as Blockchain. However, there are also many crucial distinctions between the two most popular cryptocurrencies by market capitalization. Below, we will take a closer look at the similarities and differences between Bitcoin and Ether.

KEY TIPS.

- BITCOIN MARKED the emergence of a radically new form of digital money that operates outside the control of any government or corporation.

- OVER TIME, people began to realize that one of Bitcoin's underlying innovations, the blockchain, could be used for other purposes.

- ETHEREUM PROPOSED USING Blockchain technology not only to maintain a decentralized payment network, but also to store computer code that can be used to power decentralized, tamper-proof financial applications and contracts.

- ETHEREUM APPLICATIONS and contracts run on Ether, the Ethereum network currency.

- ETHER WAS INTENDED to complement rather than compete with Bitcoin, but has nonetheless become a contender on cryptocurrency exchanges.

. . .

BITCOIN BASICS

BITCOIN WAS LAUNCHED in January 2009. It introduced a novel idea laid out in a white paper by the mysterious Satoshi Nakamoto: Bitcoin offers the promise of an online currency that is secured without any central authority, unlike government-issued currencies.

There are no physical Bitcoins, only balances associated with a cryptographically protected public ledger. Although Bitcoin was not the first attempt at such an online currency, it was the most successful in its early efforts, and has come to be known as a predecessor in some ways to virtually every cryptocurrency that has been developed over the past decade.

OVER THE YEARS, the concept of decentralized virtual currency has gained acceptance among regulators and government agencies. Although not a formally recognized means of payment or store of value, cryptocurrency has managed to carve out a niche for itself and continues to coexist with the financial system despite being regularly scrutinized and debated.

ETHEREUM BASICS

BLOCKCHAIN TECHNOLOGY IS BEING USED to create applications that go beyond just enabling a digital currency. Launched in July 2015, Ethereum is the largest and best established open decentralized software platform.

Ethereum allows the implementation of smart contracts and decentralized DApps applications to be built and run without downtime, fraud, control or interference from a third party. Ethereum comes complete with its own programming language that runs on a blockchain, allowing developers to create and run distributed applications.

ETHEREUM'S potential applications are wide-ranging and are powered by its native cryptographic token, Ether (commonly abbreviated as ETH). In 2014, Ethereum launched a presale of Ether, which received an overwhelming response. Ether is like fuel for executing commands on the Ethereum platform and developers use it to create and run applications on the platform.

ETHER IS PRIMARILY USED for two purposes: it is traded as a digital currency on exchanges in the same way as other cryptocurrencies, and it is used on the Ethereum network to run applications. According to Ethereum, "people all over the world use ETH to make payments, as a store of value or as collateral."

KEY DIFFERENCES

WHILE THE BITCOIN and Ethereum networks are based on the principle of distributed ledgers and cryptography, the two differ technically in many ways. For example, transactions on the Ethereum network can contain executable code, while the data attached to transactions on the Bitcoin network are generally just for note-keeping.

Other differences include the block time (an Ether transaction is confirmed in seconds compared to Bitcoin's minutes) and the algorithms they run on (Ethereum uses Ethash while Bitcoin uses SHA-256).

More importantly, however, the Bitcoin and Ethereum networks are different with respect to their overall goals. While Bitcoin was created as an alternative to national currencies and thus aspires to be a medium of exchange and a store of value, Ethereum was conceived as a platform to facilitate immutable, programmatic contracts and applications through its own currency.

BTC AND ETH are digital currencies, but Ether's primary purpose is not to establish itself as an alternative monetary system, but rather to facilitate and monetize the operation of the Ethereum smart contract and decentralized application platform Dapps.

ETHEREUM IS another use case for a blockchain that supports the Bitcoin network and, in theory, should not really compete with Bitcoin. However, Ether's popularity has pushed it to compete with all cryptocurrencies, especially from a merchant perspective. For most of its history since launching in mid-2015, Ether has been very close to Bitcoin in the rankings of the top cryptocurrencies by market capitalization.

That said, it is important to keep in mind that Ether's ecosystem is much smaller than Bitcoin's: as of January 2020, Ether's market cap was just under $16 billion, while Bitcoin's is nearly 10 times larger at over $147 billion.

ETHEREUM CLASSIC, **the fork of Ethereum**

ETHEREUM CLASSIC ETC, arrives to the Blockchain market one year after Ethereum was created, after the application of a Hard Fork, favored by the Ethereum community. Let's make a brief recount.

This application was activated on June 17, 2016 with the immediate purpose of recovering and solving a painful event suffered by the community, when it was the victim of a theft estimated at more than 3,600,000.00 ETH, which were and were very well safe-guarded by the project. The Decentralized Autonomous Organiza-tion (DAO), for its acronym in English, the application of this hard fork, was the one that split the Ethereum community between all those who made it up, detractors and benefactors.

Given the magnitude of this millionaire embezzlement for a little more than 56 million dollars, most of those who constituted the community gave their approval to execute this Hard Fork, which ended in a division of Ethereum in two Blockchain. Creating one that returned the stolen funds to their owners, which is now known as Ethereum, and keeping the other, the original Blockchain, where the stolen funds were not removed and in which its history continued its course with total normality. This Blockchain received the name of Ethereum Classic.

Regardless of the fact that, between these two great projects, there are marked and punctual differences that make clear many aspects for and against functions, according to the appreciation of their communities and other users; both have an interesting common factor: To become the most effective and powerful decentralized Blockchain platform in the world. Platforms with the ability to execute smart contracts without intermediaries, scam or censorship.

IN ORDER TO achieve these goals, Ethereum Classic seeks to anchor its technological system on everything it managed to inherit from Ethereum, also building its own structure backed by a commu-nity and open development, respecting the philosophical foundations of its community. Its guidelines and conditions are found in its Crypto-Decentralist Manifesto, in its Declaration of Independence where it expresses: "The Code Is The Law".

As with other cryptocurrencies, the value of each Ether is provided by the Blockchain, a constantly growing sequence of records called blocks, which are linked and secured through a crypto-graphic system. Depending on the format of its pattern, the blockchain is substantially resistant to data modification.

Ethereum Classic operates through the use of accounts and balances under a state transaction scheme unlike Bitcoin. This dynamic will not rely on the outputs of unrecorded transactions. The status expressed the current balances of each account and its additional data. The state will not be archived or stored on the blockchain, it is managed in a "Separate Merkle Patricia" tree.

All public and private keys or addresses that can be used to receive or spend Ether are stored by a cryptocurrency wallet. Ether may be generated by BIP 39-style mnemonics for an "HD wallet", BIP 32. In Ethereum technology, this is unnecessary, as it does not operate in an UTXO system. With a private key, it is quite possible to write to the Blockchain, giving effectiveness to a transaction.

TO DO ETHER TO AN ACCOUNT, the use of the Keccka-256 hash of the public key for that account is required. All Ether accounts are pseudonymous in the sense that they are not linked to particular persons, but to one or more specific addresses.

About the emergence of Ethereum Classic, whose path and existence coincides closely with Ethereum, given that both were hosted in June 2016 after the aforementioned hack of that time, it is worth noting that, among the many consequences, one was the slight but significant drop in the value of Ether and the decisive decision to sacrifice one of its most important characteristics, its "immutability". The most delicate, since most of those who made up its community at the time did not approve of this imminent exit or solution that would allow the return of illegally stolen funds.

The solution that the creator of Ethereum himself, Vitálik Buterin, proposed and about which he was in favor and convinced of its infallible effectiveness, was to initiate the reversion. Buterin wanted and formulated to extract the DAO funds safely and reliably to convert them back into Ether.

Only by initiating the reversion would the expected results be achieved. A minority of community participants did not see sacrificing the immutability of the network as the most appropriate measure. So much so that they were convinced that the best and most convenient thing to do in this situation was to continue without carrying out any type of reversion in the operations, not even in the ones that triggered the vulnerability to perpetrate the theft or the great scam to which they were being subjected.

After a breach took place in the Ethereum community, the final decision was made to trigger a Hard Fork to the Blockchain. The result was predicted and evident, a new chain was generated, having then two, which would follow their independent paths, one from the other.

The Ethereum chains, the protagonist of the hard fork, underwent an event that was believed to be almost impossible for a fraudulent situation such as the one that occurred to happen in the network.

ETHEREUM CLASSIC, which was reborn as a product of the hard fork, an alternative solution that would maintain all the original structure conceived in the creation of this platform; it guaranteed the community its essence of immutability and resistance to censorship.

THREE

SMART CONTRACTS AND THE FUTURE OF TECHNOLOGY

You are already familiar with the term, we have mentioned it on several occasions and you have read it in different paragraphs, and certain references have been made about it that give us a basic idea of what they are and their usefulness. Surely when you hear, see or read the word "contract", it comes to your mind something that represents respect constituted by a series of conditions to be fulfilled and enforced, lawyers, drafters, physical documents and number of signatures. Well, let's now see what these Smart Contracts are.

. . .

LET'S first take a brief look at their history. Between the 70's and 80's a group of computer experts and connoisseurs came up with the idea of creating and implementing new market mechanisms through a system of auctions or sales in the field of computing, as the environment to develop and present the commercial offer, a new way of selling. At the same time, Public Cryptography (cryptographic method formed by a pair of keys to share messages), was becoming a valuable ground for what would become the advanced technique on network security.

Now, the term Smart Contracts was established by computer scientist, jurist and cryptographer Nick Szabo in the early 1990s in order to accentuate and ponder its unique objective of moving what Szabo called "highly evolved" practices of contract law and related commercial exercises, towards the design of "Electronic Commerce" protocols between strangers within the virtual network; the Internet.

LONG BEFORE THE Blockchain or Blockchain appeared, there was no platform on the net that had the ability to perform or produce a smart contract, it only existed and was described conceptually. An example of what a smart contract is is Bitcoin, which is properly speaking a Smart Contracts, in which the rules of the game are clearly defined and accepted by its participants.

On the other hand, Ethereum, an important and renowned platform supports the creation of Turing Complete Smart Contracts, meaning that any program that can be created on a standard computer can be programmed here and then store the source code on the Blockchain. Under these conditions it will always be possible to create programs indefinitely, which can be executed on any computer in the network, enjoying all the benefits and advantages offered by Blockchain technology.

Precisely what Nick Szabo once considered as something indisputably non-existent in 1995, would become a reality almost 15 years later with the birth of Bitcoin in 2009 with its renowned Blockchain technology.

FACED with all these possibilities and computing opportunities, the initiative arises to continue creating; this time various programs protected and inspired by the Blockchain technology, opening the doors to a new and decentralized internet, invaded, in good measure, by a large number of applications not monitored by third parties outside the network.

The Blockchain ensures and guarantees that each and every transaction is verified and validated by multiple participants, and only those operations that follow the rules and guidelines established by a smart contract will be successfully confirmed.

THE SMART CONTRACT is like a document; a very particular and special compendium of instructions that is stored in the Blockchain. As its name says, it is "smart". It has the full capacity to execute itself in the face of actions, according to a series of patterns and parameters already programmed. Always within a secure, immutable and transparent ecosystem.

SINCE 2009, and after the launch of the first version that emerged with the creation of Bitcoin, there are many important and interesting projects that strive to provide new ideas and decentralized network solutions in favor of centralized applications used by all of us today.

ENTERING ALREADY in direct inherent content to the subject, the Smart Contracts have a basic fundamental objective, to eliminate and to leave aside all type of intermediaries in order to minimize the processes of development and execution, as well as to save significantly the relation of expenses or costs in benefit of the user.

THE BEST WAY TO understand our object of analysis, Smart Contracts, is to remember what a contract means or what a contract is.

A CONTRACT IS A WRITTEN document that will be given legality and in which a series of agreements, clauses and guidelines are established between two or more parties, which will be accepted by its participants. It will establish what can be done, how to do it and what happens if it is not done; as long as this contract is valid. A contract can be renewed. It is about respecting the rules of a game where two or more people are going to participate in conformity, after signing in acceptance of what has been previously established.

Contracts are still today, personal agreements with verbal agreements or expensive written documents, drafted by specialists in law, lawyers, notaries among others. When it comes to the written document, it will be subject to governmental and territorial laws. All of this is bundled and without number of expenses and high costs of generation, registration and validity.

A high intervention of human talent is involved in the elaboration process. For this reason they are not accessible to everyone. And on top of all this, another aspect; those typical final contents that always end up against the one who "benefits" from the contract, the characteristic small letters that can be translated, in one word: Captured!

ON THE OTHER HAND, a Smart Contract is totally independent and has the capacity to be self-executing and self-enforcing. It is a resource that works autonomously and automatically, without the participation or supervision of mediators or external agents; always and at all times avoiding the embarrassment of interpretation as it is a non-verbal element or written in native human languages.

Smart Contracts are structured in "scripts" (computer codes), written in programming language. This means that the terms established in the contract are only commands and sentences in the codes that form it. It is important that we have something very clear, and that is that a Smart Contract can be created and called by individuals or legal entities, as well as by computer programs or machines that operate autonomously and independently.

A SMART CONTRACT has and enjoys full validity without having to depend on jurisdictional authorities or legislatures. This is due to its own nature and autonomous character: It is a code that is always visible to all and that by existing on Blockchain technology, it cannot be changed or altered, it is immutable; which transfers to it a full and total profile of transparency and decentralization.

WITH THESE BASIC aspects that you have seen so far, you can imagine the great potential that a smart contract has. We highlight that, being distributed in the network by thousands of computers, it avoids bureaucracy, high costs, censorship and that these contracts are guarded by third party companies, it would be undoubtedly an arduous work and intense dedication.

IF WE WERE to take a Smart Contract with valuable and powerful foundations and merge it with a large group of outstanding developers in the world, we would have an unimaginable result, we would obtain something never seen before, something that would go beyond the limits of our own imagination. Possibilities never seen before, possible for everyone and with reduced costs. We are talking about free ecosystems without the presence of authoritarian figures demanding that the members of a virtual community act according to their will and submission. We are talking about a possible cryptodemocracy.

CONSIDER this example taken from a publication recently offered by a young man in a television interview in Bogota:

"IMAGINE A TESLA-TYPE VEHICLE, driven autonomously, that has been purchased by a group of 100 people, capable of self-managing all its services and that in turn the same vehicle rents itself. All this without having to be accountable to a Rental Cars or pay 10% of its profits to Uber".

THAT BEING THE CASE, will you join those who welcome the world of Smart Contracts?

Be careful what you think about Smart Contracts, so far .

Today, a large part of humanity is immersed in computer controls; practically everything interacts and revolves around them. In application development and planning, it is absolutely normal for developers to build a line of "gates" to each application, called APIs. These doors are open so that other programmers have the possibility of entering the application to get more information from it or create from there, much more.

In general, each web or program has its APIs, that is to say, it represents a protocol, an agreement, a contract, a recognized way in which the application is attracted to a data organization. It is through this door, by means of which a response will be obtained with the conformation of predictable data. All this, so that the communication is as effective as possible, does not fail; and with it an optimal functioning of the programs.

Such a contract, with these conditions, characteristics and freedoms is not guaranteed. It has its application server open and is controlled by some programmer or development group, who has the capacity and freedom to make changes so that, from one moment to another, everything works differently. It is a centralized contract or platform and can mutate instantaneously according to the decision and determination of a third party. This is not a Smart contract, platform, network, or application.

WE ALL NEED and require predictable, incorruptible, and transparent environments. Smart Contracts are very similar pieces of code, they have ways to call them and receive responses from them; they have a contract that is protected against damage and invasion by third parties, because they are distributed in thousands of nodes that have no way or means of altering their content. Thus, it will be possible to obtain a program that will constantly behave the same without requiring the attention and supervision of a third party.

A condition that for practically any use is really necessary. Smart Contracts, as you can see, are programs that will always behave the same and are established in the cloud, allowing and facilitating the storage and safeguarding of information and data that cannot be modified treacherously. These are the most reliable, secure and trustworthy programs that have ever been created by mankind, which only fail or give error when they have been poorly programmed.

TO CREATE or program a Smart Contract there are certain and certain secure and guaranteed steps. Let's take the example of a web page that accepts payment with cryptocurrencies, in this case Ethereum. No user or investor will want to lose their money, they will always expect a return or that the investment will generate more and more dividends.

AS A TEAM, set or group, all these qualities, in addition to providing the opportunity to build novel and valuable financial resources on the Blockchain or Blockchain, there is also the fact that each smart contract designed by programmers or programs, have the chances to innovate in the field of applications, opening the doors to probably begin to emerge even spontaneously; the first KIllers Apps or revolutionary applications in these areas that internally adjust a purchase, sale or negotiation with the use of digital currencies, depending on the situation.

THESE ARE the steps to generate a Smart Contract

A PUBLIC KEY is generated and sent between the user and the website.

2.THE FIRST TRANSACTION is created without sending it, placing as an example 3ETH in an output that the user needs the web to sign it.

3.THE USER MUST SEND the hash of the first transaction to the web page.

4.THE PORTAL WILL AUTOMATICALLY CREATE a second transaction that corresponds to the contract.

.   .   .

THE FIRST TRANSACTION is consumed in this second transaction and is returned to the user via the address provided in the first generation step. Since the first transaction requires two signatures, one by the user and one by the web portal, this operation is not yet finished and complete.

Here the next important action is the new parameter: nLock-Time. This can be added, for example, in a Bitcoin transaction, determining a future date that could well revolve around 4, 5 or 6 months. In that period, the funds cannot be incorporated into any transaction. Next, the Sequence Number of the input is also set to o. 6.

Finally, the transaction will be returned to the user unsigned. The user will check that the coins will all be returned to his possession and that everything is in perfect order. Of course, after the months stipulated with nLockTime have elapsed. As the Sequence Number is set to o, the contract can be modified in the future if the participating parties consider it necessary.

How can a user recover his funds if the website administrators disappear?

IT IS convenient to take into account that the input script (Instructions registered and recorded in each transaction) has not yet reached its end. The time span or waiting period for the user's signature still consists of a set of zeros, once the portal generated the second transaction. The only thing that would be pending would be the user's signature on the contract.

8. From this moment on, after the established months had elapsed and if both the first and second transactions were processed and the 3ETH of the first transaction were processed, they would be returned to the user in reference.

As can be seen, this is a simple, easy, practical and secure process that does not require major or difficult registration steps for the creation, follow-up and processing status.

A step-by-step procedure that generates trust and quality with the guarantee of compliance and enforcement between the parties, the agreements that will be the common thread of accurate and effective communication, sustaining over time the presence in a global network of services, beneficial, decentralized and free of high costs and operating expenses.

A BIT **about Smart Contracts in Ethereum**

ETHEREUM IS one of the most renowned and popular projects and platforms within the Smart Contracts section. It is, as we have said; a very well distributed computerized platform that is based on an open or public Blockchain, similar to Bitcoin and that also gives us the opportunity to process P2P smart contracts between nodes and without any kind of the well-known central servers in a decentralized virtual machine, the so-called EVM Ethereum Virtual Machine.

All the theory used and contained in Bitcoin, is the basis of Ethereum to be distributed. It has its own currency, its teams of miners and to top it off; its own Blockchain among many other constituent elements, but very unlike Bitcoin, Turing Completo; a novel programming language interpreter indisputably extensive is one of the most brilliant creations of Ethereum, admitting the incorporation of great complexity immersed in its Blockchain.

That is, it can easily be compared to a distributed computer, supplying and using its own currency (Ether), as the injector fuel necessary for the contract to be executed by the miners. This means that now with Ethereum every contract is now like a program with multiple functions and alternatives. However, for this case, there is something repeatedly criticized, the fact of having to create a whole new one from scratch, having to give up the Bitcoin network, the main and most powerful in the world.

EVERYTHING YOU HAVE READ, seen and heard about cryptocurrencies, Blockchain, Turing Completo, Forks, Smart Contracts, etc. exists; it is on the network and remains active in the cryptogalaxy, without being something traditionally tangible that you touch and keep in your physical wallet, or place on your desk, it exists because you see them and read them on the screen of a computer or cell phone through some application, no more from there.

Seeing how the crypto world and its dynamics practically move dreams, ideas, projects, change lifestyles and the economy of the planet, generating knowledge and developing intelligence; it is up to us to imagine the infinity of leaps and movements, twists and sociocultural transformations that will gradually give our daily life and way of seeing things, even the daily occurrence from home to work, as in the sciences and arts of the world.

Imagine a group of investors planning urban plans in the coming years and designing their Smart Contracts to define sales plans and their reinvestment of funds in favor of new shares.

In this way, interested parties would buy through Blockchain technology and the possession of their assets covered by Smart Contracts. This would guarantee that each unit built and sold would have transparency and due monitoring in the management of expenses.

THIS WOULD BE a new way of selling real estate and an innovation in the real estate world.

AS YOU HAVE BEEN able to verify and see so far, there are many technological platforms that go together in a race towards excellence, seeking to provide the best alternative in high-end technological solutions in an environment of constant creativity, where all go with a common goal and purpose: To make friction points in traditional operating systems decline, ensuring with their proposals to save time and money in favor of people, prospects and users.

FOUR

UNDERSTANDING DAPPS

DApps (Decentralized Applications) are simply decentralized applications. It is an application style that has a functionality based, as its name suggests, on decentralized networks of nodes all interacting with each other within the network. If we talk about decentralized applications, it is because there are also centralized applications.

Centralized applications are those that we frequently use from the Internet and are controlled by a single or central entity, a person or group, an institution or a company, through which all its functions, protocols and operating systems hosted on its servers are governed and regulated. This entity has total control of the architecture that makes up the application. The centralized application will enjoy prestige, recognition and acceptance only if the users support it. A clear example of a centralized application is a bank.

DApps, on the other hand, are applications that do not depend on being instrumented by monitored control points or central servers, but operate on the basis of a decentralized network distributed worldwide. A network over which its users and subscribers are in full control.

DApps allow users to access all their services in a reliable and secure way. These DApps can be used from the web, through a cell phone or through a computer.

LET'S clarify a little more what DApps are, for this we will represent the explanation with examples of common and already traditional names of applications and that perhaps at this precise moment you are using. In the category of traditional applications we have to mention without a doubt Facebook, YouTube, Instagram and Twitter. In these apps and also social networks, data and information as well as decisions are made on their central servers.

This gives the company behind the name, the power to sanction, limit and censor content, affecting negatively or benefiting others according to their particular considerations, with which they could put before a condition of judgment to users or followers that could be affected by some measure taken arbitrarily and that according to the rules and conditions of the centralized application, should not happen; publish or transmit inappropriate or inappropriate content that violates the rules.

The existence of DApps is not something new or recent. Initially, DApps became known in file sharing protocols, such as DC++ or BitTorrent, Peer-To-Peer system applications with file sharing features with high resistance to censorship. Always maintaining a relevant position in the network, is Bitcoin digital platform, being the first DApp using Blockchain. This fact stands out because its structure and operation successfully describe the first Blockchain DApp in history.

Arriving in 2014 and then with the presentation of the Ethereum project and its Solidity language along with the ability to execute Smart Contracts, DApps grew in mass. Fortunately this triad allowed DApps, running on the Blockchain; to gain more popularity. A timely situation that could well drive mass adoption of Blockchain as a cutting-edge technology, bringing new ways of interaction between users, real and virtual world.

BROADENING the conceptual spectrum of DApps and trying to know them a little more, let's look at some differences of interest between a DApp and traditional App, keeping in mind that both have many elements in common. However, the main differences lie in what and how these elements interact with each other.

These applications have three fundamental conditions or structures:

Frontend, backend and data storage layer.

FRONTEND

THIS IS the first layer of the structure. It is the interface used by users and through which they interact with the application. This is the case in which both DApps and traditional Apps are free to make use of the immensity of graphic resources available for this purpose.

This ranges from web interfaces developed in HTML5 scripting to more elaborate ones in greater detail, in frameworks such as Qt or GTK. The simple purpose of this first layer is to give the user the opportunity to interact by sending and receiving information with the application being used.

· · ·

BACKEND

IT IS the second layer of the structure. The purpose of this layer is to refer to the main logic of the application. For a traditional application, it is centralized logic, unlike DApps for which its logic is decentralized.

In DApps, the backend is closely related to a Smart Contract, since it runs on a Blockchain. As an example we have the case of Ethereum. Here it is demonstrated how a Smart Contract has a programming that guarantees the optimal operation of the DApp. As Smart Contracts are visible and public, a sufficiently high level of transparency and security is guaranteed. Users and participants can feel confident that the DApp will not take arbitrary actions or do anything different from what was agreed and specified in the Smart Contract.

On another note, we should add that the backend is supported by APIs (Application Programming Interface) and Blockchain capabilities. Various APIs are hosted in Ethereum that serve to control the interaction of its users or subscribers with the storage or authentication layers.

DATA STORAGE LAYER

THIS IS THE THIRD LAYER. For traditional applications, this is also a centralized layer. Data is usually stored on the user's computer and also on servers that are controlled by third party entities, individuals or companies.

This working structure, unfortunately, presents a large number with many points of failure. For example, a user could lose all the base information he has stored on the application in case his computer gets damaged.

. . .

ANOTHER SITUATION COULD BE that in any and all circumstances beyond the user's control, the servers are out of service or are surprisingly blocked. All these situations would limit and prevent the user from being able to use the application correctly, in addition to running the risk of losing any or all of the information.

For DApps, data storage is completely decentralized. All DApp users will be able to store their complete history of actions performed in the DApp network. In addition to that, all interactions will be stored on the Blockchain internally in the Blockchain blocks.

All these steps are cryptographically secure, preventing unauthorized access by third parties. Thus, if a user's computer or Smartphone were to be damaged, it would be enough to use the DApp in any other or a new device to recover and save all the information up to that precise moment of the event.

Add to this, that the level of redundancy and security with the data, is growing as the average increases and so there are more and new users making and giving use to the DApp.

HOW DAPPS WORK

A DAPP WORKS VERY MUCH like a Blockchain network. In this sense, each user of the DApp represents a node within the same network. Each user will be the guarantor of the proper and correct functioning of the operations performed in the same network.

AS WE ALREADY KNOW, the channel or means of communication used by the DApp is the Blockchain. In this blockchain, there is a record of each operation and transaction that transits through the Smart Contract controlled by the DApp. The acceptance or non-approval of the operations carried out by the DApp users is subject to the programming of the Smart Contract in question. In this way, it is intended to seek the best and most reliable guarantee in the network, so that all participants and users act within the framework specified by it.

The Smart Contract or smart contract in this case, is the intermediate point that is responsible for checking the validity of each interaction. Whenever a new transaction occurs in the DApp, the platform information will be updated in each of the nodes. In this way, it can be guaranteed that all the data is properly stored in each of them. Only in this way, each user makes his contribution in keeping the application upright with all the resources of his computer.

This preparation also guarantees and takes for granted that the platform will always be in operation and service. All this due to the impossibility of terminating all the nodes of the network at the same time. This situation or act could very well happen and be due to a computer attack or for other reasons such as censorship.

IT IS HERE where DApps have a great advance and a very marked advantage, since, by the fact of working and running directly on a Blockchain, they enjoy its benefits and capabilities of security, privacy and even; an even greater one: anonymity. Additionally, DApps also have the power to guarantee that the data used by them is only accessible by the person or user who originated or generated such information. Thus, those who use DApps will maintain absolute and firm control of their data at all times.

DAPPS AND THEIR CHARACTERISTICS:

SECURITY

. . .

SECURITY REPRESENTS the main characteristic of DApps. Thanks to the fact that they work and operate directly on the functionality of the Blockchain, which uses hard cryptography, they are able to secure the data they handle.

This aspect, which gives robustness to the DApp, ensures that all information can only be seen by those who originate or create it, the rest of those who participate will only have access or the possibility to verify and corroborate its validity or disapproval. The information generated by one user is never visible to another, never to a third party.

IN ADDITION TO THE ABOVE, all data handled by the application will at all times be under the possession and control of the user. DApps do not save or store information in the cloud or on external servers. This is an excellent option to minimize the risks associated with the theft of identities and private information or the sale of the same on behalf of the company, thus violating the privacy of its users.

DECENTRALIZATION

ONE OF THE main characteristics of DApps is that they are decentralized. In other words, the ability to operate without supervised central servers.

To place ourselves in a better context or in greater perspective, let's consider the following example: Facebook. One of the most used social networks and with more followers worldwide. With more than 2.74 billion users, its data centers and data centers handle a titanic load of information.

In this sense, maintaining the infrastructure of its platform in operation and service is a colossal task. An application that has not been exempt from crashes and errors, which have caused the network to be inoperative and out of service on a global scale. All this happens simply because Facebook is a centralized social network.

A DAPP IS free from this point of failure thanks to the quality of decentralization. Each of the DApp users has its own complete history of all actions taken on the DApp. Something like a global replica or recording of everything that has happened in the application.

Due to this, and to the fact that its execution is hosted on a Blockchain, it is sufficient for a single user to be active for the network to continue its operation without setbacks or problems. In this way, it is fully guaranteed that the DApp and its network will work perfectly and will not experience a global crash as it usually happens with Facebook.

OPEN SOURCE

IT TURNS out to be a fairly common feature that DApps have. The fact that the source code of an application is available, is a guarantee of a very high level of transparency for DApps. This is because the community will always be able to see what the DApp is doing.

A DApp as a decentralized application will always be able to allow community audits, so that anyone with the necessary knowledge will have the power and freedom to review the application's source code. This is something that will allow to improve it and, in any case, to give continuity to its development, if for any reason the project is abandoned by its original creators.

. . .

EACH AND EVERY one of the DApps keeps its source code subscribed in its Smart Contracts and the other parts of the application in a firm and public form. In this way, anyone can examine the source code, improve it or fork it directly.

BLOCKCHAIN INHERITANCE

DAPPS INTERACT DIRECTLY on the Blockchain from which their own Smart Contract is executed. This means, that each interaction on the DApp generates its own data entry on the Blockchain. This data is then stored cryptographically to give it transparency and security. All these actions can be publicly reviewed in the block explorer of the Blockchain.

Only cryptographic interactions can be seen, the entire data is stored cryptographically as we have indicated on several occasions, all in a secure manner. In addition to this, and the fact that a DApp works on a Blockchain or Blockchain, indicates that a consensus protocol will be used for verification and verification of each interaction.

Here the Proof of Work (PoW) or Proof of Stake (PoS) is applied, otherwise, whichever one the DApp developer chooses. Only with this will it be possible to guarantee the same level of security that must be applied to the Blockchain over the DApp.

Classification of DApps According to the current dynamics, DApps can be classified into three categories. These are:

DApps

TYPE I DAPPS

. . .

IN THE TYPE I CLASSIFICATION, all those DApps whose blockchain or Blockchain is their own are grouped together. That is, those that have their own construction and do not depend on any other Blockchain to run. In this sense, Bitcoin is recognized as the first Blockchain DApp in itself that has ever existed. This is a condition that also applies to Bitcoin Cash, Litecoin, Ethereum, Dash, Monero, among many others.

Type II DApps

IN THE TYPE II CLASSIFICATION, we group and we find all those DApps that will depend on an external Blockchain and its own characteristics to function and thus run. In this sense, these DApps can operate using their own tokens or those of the Blockchain on which they are being supported to run. An example in this type of classification can be found in Golem.

GOLEM IS A DAPP THAT, in order to run, relies on the Ethereum Blockchain. Golem was created with the purpose of allowing all its users to rent computing resources and implements for data processing and to be applied in different uses. Imagine Golem as a large decentralized supercomputer on which we can rent "processing power".

In order to achieve and deliver this, Golem has an ERC-20 token, the GNT (Golem Network Token). This token is used to make payments to users who rent their computing power and for other types of activities within the network.

Type III DApps

. . .

THE TYPE III classification groups together those DApps that use the Type II group of DApps for their execution and operation. In general, Type III DApps use the tokens of Type II DApps to perform their operations.

An example of these DApps leveraged on Type II DApps is Safe Network. Safe Network is a DApp that relies on Omni Layer, a Type II DApp, dedicated to generate the Safecoin, its native cryptocurrency. Its cryptocurrency, Safecoin, is used in the Safe Network DApp in order to perform all the operations available within this DApp.

SOME LIMITATIONS IN DAPPS.

- LEVEL OF DIFFICULTY in exploiting the full potential of the hardware in their users' devices.

- THE LEVEL of complexity in the application can occasionally make debugging and security review difficult.

- SUPEDED DEVELOPMENT of DApps according to the enrichment of updates within the Blockchain structure.

- CONFLICT TO IMPLEMENT functionalities necessary for the correct development of DApps.

The most popular DApps

CryptoKitties

· · ·

LAUNCHED as one of the world's pioneer games created based on Blockchain technology. CryptoKitties is dedicated to collecting "unique virtual kittens". Each of the offered and collectible kitties has its own characteristics and properties that make them different from each other. The extreme rarity represented in this DApp is what gives it so much value and makes it the cryptocurrency of the game.

The user can buy the kittens which can also be sold, thus receiving their ownership virtually. In addition, with these kittens you have the option of making a family, you can already "breed" kittens in CryptoKitties. For this you will only have to join a pair of kittens to create a unique genetic offspring, which you will keep, breed later or sell to make your digital feline business.

CryptoKitties runs on top of the Ethereum Blockchain, and is a Type II DApp.

NASH

LIKE CRYPTOKITTIES, Nash is a Type II DApp and one that requires the NEO Blockchain to run. The main goal conceived by Nash, is to run an Off-Chain matching engine that allows in the user much more effective, fast and complex exchanges to existing decentralized exchanges.

Saturn Network Saturn Network is a decentralized exchange DApp for trading ERC-20 or ERC-223 tokens. Its operation is based on a Cross-Chain that is available on both Ethereum and Ethereum Classic.

Saturn Network offers the network, an expedited and effortless exchange system, as it does not require or need to fill out a KYC or perform any account setup.

Crazy Dogs Live

. . .

CRAZY DOGS LIVE DApp is a gaming and betting system focused on creating a transparent, fun and secure platform for its users and the community in general. Crazy Dogs Live is among the dog races and competitions with a set of innovative betting mining and live streaming features.

Crazy Dogs Live allows players to interact with each other in a fun and entertaining gaming activity, while also earning winnings. The platform is in the process of designing and planning its next release with new features in the near future so that the entire gaming ecosystem will grow exponentially.

Crazy Dogs Live is a Type II DApp running on top of the TRON Blockchain.

"With this new technology in the wild, some people might feel electrified by the idea of decentralizing all things."

ALL OF US who currently use the Internet have no control over the data we usually view, see and share on the web. Among the many existing platforms, Ethereum is considered by many experts as the only one that adds efforts and tries to manage its Blockchain as a way to improve what its designers consider to be a part of the problematic design of the Internet.

LET'S keep in mind that decentralized DApps, are applications executable on a P2P network of computers rather than a single one. DApps have been around since P2P networks first appeared. These applications are designed in a style of software programs designed to coexist and be hosted on the Internet in a way that is not monitored and controlled by a single entity.

. . .

THESE DAPPS-TYPE APPLICATIONS managed to establish themselves as a way to reduce the impact and action of third parties on an application's own functions; they simply connect their users and providers directly.

An interesting and illustrative case of the use of DApps for social networks would be for example for a decentralized and censorship-resistant Instagram. That is, once you publish a post on its Blockchain, it cannot be deleted even by the company that created the microblogging system.

UNLIKE TRADITIONAL CENTRALIZED APPLICATIONS, where the backend code runs on centralized servers, DApps have their own backend code in a decentralized P2P network and are accessed from there through the well-known Smart Contract.

DAPPS ARE THEREFORE DECENTRALIZED applications that use the Blockchain to run and in turn all its users relate directly and reliably among themselves, to close agreements of their convenience without a central entity that manages, censures, supervises or monitors the service.

FIVE

CRYPTOCURRENCY ICOS

Initial Coin Offer (ICO)

Initial Coin Offering; are in the world of cryptocurrencies a revolution in corporate financing around the world, using all the strength that deploys its technology based on the Blockchain.

ICOs make it possible to achieve financing to materialize large short-term projects in a reliable, fast and simple way. Within the spectrum represented by the cryptomundo, ICOs are much more than feasible resources for financing, they are a powerful tool in favor of all types of investment.

Imagine again that group of people who got together and invested to buy the Tesla self-driving car, bring them back to your mind and get in the mood for financing this initiative. Thanks to ICOs, all this is possible. An ICO is a financial instrument or resource that makes this type of plans and projects a reality, where it is very attractive, as it does not involve the usual administrative and legal bureaucracy that we are already familiar with and that traditional financing methods entail.

ICOS ARE a new type or model of collective or group financing that is taken hand in hand with Blockchain technology. A modality that revolutionizes the planet as a whole and the crypto-world, producing profits that exceed 50,000% in certain cryptocurrency ICOs.

BY MEANS OF AN ICO, what is sought is the financing of an initiative through the issuance of a currency from the blockchain, Blockchain technology, cryptocurrencies. The exchange with these cryptocurrencies, like the existing ones, can be carried out without major complications. They can also be bought and sold freely, with the market itself, through its users, setting their placement price as a basis for supply and demand. This means that, if you buy at a certain price and manage to sell at a higher one, you will make an interesting profit and benefit from the operation carried out.

ICOs are a resource that is gaining ground and is present daily within the various operational actions in the network and its entire community, allowing economic support as part of interesting projects that are supported among users, who understand their weighting and the benefits that can be achieved through them.

Let's know more in detail what cryptocurrency ICOs are, and for that purpose, we must start from their bases, from the beginning. To do so, we must know and understand what is traditionally a financing and then describe in detail, what is an ICO? Including advantages, examples and precautions among many other aspects. This way we will know a little more about what this evolution in the world of cryptocurrencies means.

FINANCE **1.0**

LET'S start by getting to know a little about financing, in particular Financing 1.0. Nowadays, in addition to initiatives, we talk about ventures, which grow in times of crisis.

In order to implement and materialize these ideas or concerns, an important economic contribution or investment will always be necessary. In any aspect or moment of the initiative, we will be subject to a series of necessary expenses, no matter how small or big they may be, money will be imperatively necessary.

FROM THE TRADITIONAL AND CULTURAL, before the lack or requirement of personal or business economic resources, the solution to cover these expenses, has been present thanks to one or a combination of the following three ways: Financing by loan application, financing by subsidy (granting of money) and financing by sale of shares.

The basic character of this financing model consists of borrowing money. These loans are usually requested or requested to any person or entity that is in the capacity to cover this request. It is therefore, as said; individuals or companies, financial institutions, banks or even government institutions, among many other options. The most common prototype for this type of financing is the following:

YOU RECEIVE as a loan an amount X of money that you will have to pay back in Y period of time, paying an interest of Z% per month.

The interest represents the profit that the lender acquires from the negotiation.

Under this financing format you do not grant any type or amount of shares of your company for negotiation. With this loan application you can achieve a financing that will allow you to develop the product to revalue the company. That is, a way to revalue all the shares of the organization or project.

Grant financing (Grant money)

GRANT FINANCING MAY or may not be associated with a loan itself. Grant financing is usually provided by government agencies and is usually not subject to a condition of repayment or interest charges.

BY MEANS OF A GRANT, the entrepreneur or the company will not deliver any shares or shared assets resulting from the company's activity.

ONE OF THE most common and traditional procedures used to achieve the financing of a project, let's call it that, is the sale of shares. These sales are made privately among relatives, friends or prominent investors or by means of an Initial Public Offering (IPO). In this type of sale, the entrepreneur could start his initiative, capturing the interest of other people with whom he would share part of his project through the shares.

By means of the Public Offering of Sale (IPO), a company, for example, may apply for 1,000 shares that will be bought at the initial moment at a determined price. In this way, the company has already financed itself through the placement and trading of these shares. These shares are a representation of the participation in the company and also of its own profits.

When a company's productive and commercial activity is running and looking good, it earns more money and therefore its shares grow in value over time. This will allow the shares to generate large and important dividends, which means, in turn, that the company will grant the corresponding part of its profits to each of its shareholders on a regular basis.

THESE ARE the reasons why there will always be people (investors) interested in acquiring or buying shares at a price even higher than the starting price. Then, the person who has bought a certain amount of shares will be free to exchange them for other goods, services, fiat money or cryptocurrencies to other interested buyers. The investor who sells his acquired shares at a certain value will see profits if he makes the transaction at a higher price than the initial purchase price.

FINANCE **2.0**

IN ORDER TO go public and participate in the stock market, huge and high requirements must be met, which is often a major problem for companies. This is why, in the face of these strong and closed application requirements, creativity was given the opportunity again and thus the already very popular term Crowdfunding (2006), which is a fundraising, came into being a few years ago.

THIS ACTIVITY ALREADY EXISTED, only that the word "crowd-funding" appears for the first time and according to records, in an article published by Michael Sullivan in his blog "fundavlog", on August 12, 2006.

Taking a brief look at history, we could say that Alexander Pope (1688), a famous English poet, was translating into English the masterpiece of Greek literature "The Iliad" by Homer. Alexander did not have the economic funds or the money necessary for such work. For this reason, a very creative fundraising campaign was devised to solve his problem.

Alexander Pope offered people the possibility of investing a certain amount of money to help him publish the first volume and then receive a copy once the work was finished, something like a pre-sale.

POPE CREATED a simple campaign with the following words: "This Work will be printed in six volumes, on the finest paper; with ornaments and initial letters engraved in Copper".

PARTICIPATING 750 people were his backers and all were greeted with their names on the manuscript. This is perhaps the first "reward" commercial project in history to be crowdfunded.

LET'S return to our moment in time, year 2021 and continue to offer details about crowdfunding.

CROWDFUNDING IS one of the many ways used to raise money and other resources through a network of people, called patrons. In order to obtain the funds or resources, a period of time is determined, which is usually one month, and it is during this period when the money must be raised. This is money that should be used to finance the project, however, there is no guarantee that this will actually be the case.

Every day we see more and more websites dedicated to the creation of crowdfunding. This happens because the Internet allows more people around the world to have the opportunity to promote their projects with the aim of financing them with people interested in supporting them.

ALTHOUGH THERE ARE many types of crowdfunding on donations, rewards, shares, loans, royalties, etc. that we could find on the web, it is very normal that, due to bureaucracy and high costs, investments are considered or taken simply as donations with the expectation of receiving some discount, recognition or other type of benefit.

ICOS ARE HERE - **Financing 3.0**

ICO IS in the Blockchain crypto world, the raising and attraction of funding through the sale of a cryptocurrency. ICO, Initial Coin Offering for its acronym in English, is Initial Coin Offering.

ICOS GIVE a flight of freedom to the financing of initiatives, ideas or projects. And that flight is given by allowing anyone in the world to apply to fund or finance an idea in just a few seconds. As a result, whoever proposes the project will receive a digital asset that is easy to trade, highlighting the image of a close, united and borderless global world.

An ICO does not mean or pretend to imply the creation of a cryptocurrency. It never represents a previous mining work, neither issuing it, and much less creating a Smart Contract or Colored Coin. Everything turns out to be indifferent and may even and may never have coexisted with an ICO. An ICO is the process by which a cryptocurrency is distributed and deployed, usually by cashing a cryptocurrency at an early stage of development of some activity or initiative. This digital currency may be used in the project, and thus, achieve the goal of financing such development, program or plan.

. . .

SUCH IS the steady and effective growth that cryptocurrency ICOs and other Blockchain projects have experienced and continue to represent, that the investments raised by companies demonstrably exceed the typical traditional investment raised from all StartUps.

MANY CRYPTOCURRENCIES CONTINUE to emerge since the birth of Bitcoin, the forerunner of this movement. There are thousands of thousands, but their emergence and the way they have been appearing varies significantly from one to another.

Since 2009, when Bitcoin became active, and until 2014, in general terms, the trend was for new cryptocurrencies to base their activity on an issue associated with an algorithm. Let's see, for example, the PoW (Proof of Work) or PoS (Proof of Stake) algorithm. At this point, PoW is the most common as it is the format used by Bitcoin and practically by the vast majority of existing cryptocurrencies.

CRYPTOCURRENCIES THAT ARE BASED on PoW or PoS support a free form of distribution of the total cryptocurrencies that are mined, which appear in the distribution period. Very much in the distance of the advantages and disadvantages of each algorithm, the reality is that in them there is no centralized entity that is in charge of issuing the new cryptocurrencies, on the contrary, these are mined. This is due to the presence or existence of a program with certain clear rules for the whole community, which allows the mining of the coins, not their issuance, and that in turn there is competition for it.

IT WAS INTENDED that all this would change gradually and gradually. By 2013 the first initiatives came to light that, although before making the software of digital currencies public, their promoters and developers are responsible for mining them in advance and in private mode. This was a quite practical way of financing themselves in the future. This action was known as pre-mining of coins or pre-mined coins.

IN THESE PRE-MINED COIN OPERATIONS, the promoters and developers kept a large part of the coins for themselves for later. In this way, and once the coin began to trade, they could sell it and thus recover their previous investment and sometimes even become rich.

This type of activities and practices were associated with strong and harsh criticism from the community. Because they were based on clear and evident disadvantageous environments, these pre-mining exercises were associated with unfair models.

ETHEREUM APPEARED IN 2014, and with its arrival on the cryptographic network would not only seek an effective redefinition of Blockchain technology, but also of traditional financing systems. This Ethereum did: it mined its coins in advance. This as a root cause to the fact that the project would not go live until at least a little over 1 year later.

All the coins produced from pre-mining, instead of being saved or stored were put up for sale in order to fund the later phase of the work. Ethereum was not the first to try to sell its cryptocurrencies, as one of the first cryptocurrency ICOs had just appeared. Thanks to this action Ethereum was able to capitalize an approximate collection of 19 million dollars in Bitcoins.

IN THE MIDDLE of the first decade of the 2000s, the cryptocurrencies that appeared went from being cryptocurrencies with generation supported by competition, to digital currencies with a format in which the promoters of a project were careful to sell their cryptocurrencies that they had mined with obvious advantageous environments, before any host of the crypto network could compete with them.

UNTIL 2014, practically all the cryptocurrencies that emerged were coins that in some way or another sought to oppose or compete with Bitcoin or contributed with some major change in terms of protocol. The conception of a new cryptocurrency was not fundamentally based on converting it or using it as a single payment instrument or resource in a web or application where the environment was very limited.

THE UNSTOPPABLE ICO cryptocurrency revolution brought about an imminent total change. From now on cryptocurrencies would be created for every type of market, literally for anything. In this way it was admitted to be more evident than ever that cryptocurrencies could be considered as valid digital assets. Now we would speak of cryptoassets: tokens with all the necessary conditions to represent a value that could flow with the same speed, ease and security as a known cryptocurrency.

FROM ANYWHERE IN THE WORLD, sitting in the front row and in the first person, we were witnessing and observing with full clarity the scenario of the birth and welcoming of the Internet of Value. From now on and with this new token model, any idea that came to our minds could use this technique and pattern to finance itself in a comfortable and always reliable way. All this and much more by offering, for example, a token that would allow a certain, certain or such a service within the future implementation of the idea or initiative in question, for example.

. . .

THE CASES that have taken this technique as a use model are varied and the creativity is simply unstoppable. With all these elements, a set of incentives is constituted that are very similar to stocks, the more demanded the service or product to which this new cryptocurrency has been linked or the more attractive the cryptocurrency's own characteristics are, the higher its price or value will be due to the demand.

Let's remember what we talked about in chapter 3 dedicated to Smart Contracts, with a Smart Contract or smart contract can interact people, users or companies, and in the same way other Smart Contracts and even machines. That is why, based on such good results and positive consequences of Smart Contracts, cryptocurrency ICOs are created.

You've thought about it, haven't you, and the answer is probably yes. The same machines could even create and launch cryptocurrency ICOs that other machines would fund among themselves, all this by self-execution. And I repeat, these scenarios are possible and believably something totally normal in the not too distant future, thanks to the technological evolution of the network. The intelligence in the network does not rest.

ETHEREUM TOKENS

BEFORE KNOWING what Ethereum tokens are, let's refresh some concepts that, although we have already seen them, it is appropriate to review them again.

Ethereum is, as you already know; a decentralized platform in which Smart Contracts are executed, which makes it clear that Ethereum is not a cryptocurrency. Ethereum's native digital currency is Ether. If someone sells a vehicle, the seller will receive the respective funds, the buyer will receive the vehicle and its right of owner-ship; all these steps of corresponding transfers can be well performed by Ethereum, thanks to its open source system and other important resources.

ON THE OTHER HAND, we have tokens. A token is defined as a "something" that has the quality and characteristic of representing another. Within the blockchain or Blockchain, a token usually repre-sents a financial value or a digital asset. Tokens are like gambling chips in a casino. They represent fiat money for use in gaming and slot machines, which is then exchanged for physical money.

NOW, we have already remembered and clarified the two main differences between Ethereum and tokens, and we must also add that both are simply digital assets that are created at the closing of a blockchain. On the other hand, tokens are ready to fulfill the great job of strengthening the ecosystem by boosting the demand for Ether in the best way, as already mentioned; Ethereum's native currency.

THE ETHEREUM TOKEN, just like all the systems and elements that make up the network, has its identity, and it is ERC20, so talking about ERC20 token or simply ERC20, should already sound familiar to you.

ERC20 token

ERC STANDS for Ethereum Requests for Comments (ERC), while the number 20 comes from the Ethereum Improvement Proposal (EIP), which is where it is described. So, ERC20 is a standard interface in charge of ensuring interoperability between each of the tokens.

Now, ERC20 tokens are a subset of Ethereum tokens that are adjusted and complemented to meet certain and certain parameters. To properly perform its functions as an ERC20, its developers must set it up in its conformation, a specific set of functions set forth in its Smart Contract that, at a high-end level, will give it authority to accomplish the following actions:

- OBTAIN the full supply of tokens.

- OBTAIN THE ACCOUNT balance

- TRANSFER the token

- APPROVE TOKEN SPENDING Thanks to the functions assigned to the ERC20 interface, Smart Contracts can be used for the following actions

ERC20, Smart Contracts and DApps on the Ethereum Blockchain; it enjoys seamless interaction with them. Moreover, tokens with some of the standard functions (not all), are considered to be limitedly related to ERC20 and still could interact according to restriction of their own functions.

Generally speaking, an ERC20 token itself does not represent much difference from any other token, but also conforms to the standard Ethereum token.

. . .

ETHEREUM NEEDS **a standard token**

IF ALL TOKENS that have so far been created within the same Ethereum network used the same standard, exchanging them would simply be easy and they would have the power to work and run immediately with DApps compatible with the use of the standard ERC20 interface.

A token is standardized when it uses a specific set or number of functions. Knowing in advance how a token will work, its developers can integrate it into their projects with the assurance that it will work properly and without any fear of making mistakes. If a set of tokens exhibit the same behavior, calling exactly the same functions, then a DApp will be able to interact much more easily with different sub-currencies.

On par with Bitcoin and Ether, Ethereum's ERC20 tokens can be tracked on the Blockchain, the public ledger of record of each and every transaction and operation produced. This is possible, as Ethereum tokens represent a unique and specific type of Smart Contract or smart contract that inhabits the Ethereum Blockchain.

Currently the number of projects leveraged on the Ethereum Blockchain is increasing as they are also on the ERC20 interface standard for issuing tokens to operate their respective platforms. The likelihood that this market will continue to grow rapidly with new and effective applications designed to fulfill key functions to interact with each other, are the order of the day. And all the platforms are projecting themselves towards that goal.

SIX

ETHEREUM 2.0, THE FUTURE

After several years, the long-awaited Ethereum 2.0 is finally here. The crypto community joyfully celebrated what will very soon be the new network and ETH has now returned to its ATH. But what is Ethereum 2.0 and why is it important?

Ethereum was a huge success in 2015. Vitálik Buterin and his team have introduced a revolutionary smart contract ecosystem to the Blockchain industry, which soon became a universe of its own within the cryptocurrency market.

Every developer wanted to create a decentralized application on Ethereum, and the only way to do so was by Crowdfunding through token sales. Almost instantly, Initial Coin Offerings (ICOs) started an investment craze that catapulted cryptocurrencies to new heights.

Cryptocurrency veterans have thoroughly enjoyed this period. But even in 2015, they knew Ethereum still had a long way to go before reaching its full potential. A blockchain dedicated to both smart contracts and DApps can only serve a certain number of users and, at a certain point, it will reach a bottleneck that will hinder all future growth.

TO GET RID of this limitation, the Ethereum Foundation announced that it plans to migrate from Proof of Work to Proof of Stake. The new update to the network redefines how nodes validate blocks while taking scalability to an unprecedented level.

WHAT IS ETHEREUM 2.0?

YOU ALREADY KNOW **all about Ethereum, but what about Ethereum 2.0?**

THE TECHNICAL DETAILS can be a bit complicated, but the mission of the new network is pretty straightforward.

ETHEREUM 2.0 IS BASED on PoS (Proof-of-Stake), a consensus mechanism in which nodes validate transactions and blocks by staking tokens. In this case, anyone can participate in the network and run a node by depositing and blocking 32 ETH.

. . .

EACH NODE HAS the ability to be selected by the network, which entitles it to propose a block. While the process is a bit random compared to Proof of Work, users who have a higher amount of assets still have a higher chance of winning. If the node successfully completes the task, the node owner earns money for both proposing the block and verifying it.

Developers have spent years trying to figure out how to implement Proof of Stake in a practical way. The Ethereum team created and scraped roadmaps on a regular basis, which left them with a bad reputation that still haunts them to this day.

HOWEVER, things had changed for the better in 2019 when the Ethereum Foundation finally figured out a solution that works. Not only did they have to figure out how to create Ethereum 2.0, but they also had to come up with a plan on how to launch the new network without killing the old one.

ETHEREUM **2.0 vs. Ethereum**

WE ARE CURRENTLY in the era of Ethereum 1.0 and the platform has become the undisputed holder of a second position that it maintains and occupies at will, always under the shadow of Bitcoin, a situation that is intended to change, trying to give Ethereum all the elements that will propel it to become a much more influential reference behind a future new version.

THE ETHEREUM we know is the one we essentially mine, but a new version Ethereum 2.0 is coming, which sounds more like the one that is coming, Ethereum 1.5 which has not generated the hype that already has us in the environment the possibility of ending Ethereum mining in the very short term.

The purpose of Ethereum 2.0 "Serenity" the future new interaction of the platform alongside its native currency, the Ether. This new version will be reborn with a revamped blockchain or Blockchain improving the comprehensive efficiency of the system, the number of transactions per second for payments, scalability and the disappearance of its greatest charm: Ethereum's blockchain mining with GPUs.

WELL IT IS worth noting that Ethereum is not the only cryptocurrency on the network struggling to beat scalability, they all do so by each applying their own strategies. Ethereum has prepared a terrain of impact with its 2.0 version, which makes the future look uncertain for the platform, its components and especially for the community. Many are even wondering if there will be two Ether with different values. Thus, any number of concerns.

THE ETHEREUM 2.0 Serenity version is still in full development phase and therefore we have not yet been announced a precise or approximate release date, however, enough information about this new version is flowing, as to transmit it from now and go knowing little by little on the subject.

Let's say that the main difference between Ethereum 1.0 and Ethereum 2.0 lies in its consensus mechanism, which allows you to add or incorporate new blocks to the blockchain. While version 1.0 uses a Proof of Work (PoW), the future version will use a Proof of Stake (PoS).

THE PROGRAMMERS responsible for this modification and the renewed blockchain also emphasize and highlight that the issue of security will also be sighted as a vital point and will be much higher. Ethereum 2.0 requires a minimum of 16,384 validators for each operation or transaction, a higher number than many other PoS networks. The decentralization is also much greater, and so is the security achieved with this new proposal, although it also has its doubts about potential problems and conflicts of interest to be resolved.

At the moment the climate around the Ethereum 2.0 version appears optimistic and promising for its developers, full of effective and very positive expectations, but still in full development. In fact, different phases have been put forward to reach a fully firm and guaranteed Ethereum 2.0:

PHASE 0:

THE NEW BEACONCHAIN is implemented to store and manage the validator registry and the PoS consensus mechanism. For the time being the original Ethereum 1.0 PoW blockchain will remain active so that data continuity exists.

PHASE 1:

BY 2021 IT is estimated that a new stage in the network will be reached and begin to be deployed, initially with 64 times the capacity and transactions per second of the current network. Subsequently, and also expected by 2021, the network will become fully effective and the PoS consensus will be definitively transitioned.

PHASE 1.5:

.   .   .

AN INTERIM UPDATE expected by 2021 as its likely date, Ethereum's MainNet will officially become a shard of the Blockchain and transition to Proof of Stake (PoS).

PHASE 2:

BY THE END of 2021 or perhaps as early as 2022, the new blockchain is estimated to be fully functional and compatible with Smart Contracts. This will make it possible to include Ether accounts and enable both cryptocurrency transfers and withdrawals.

THE FUTURE for Ethereum 2.0 is therefore quite promising for a blockchain that as mentioned has only just been born and still needs to complete a transition period that will have an estimated duration of more than a year. Experts believe that these changes will undeniably boost the value of Ether and Ethereum.

We'll see if indeed it does and if this platform manages to become a much more palpable benchmark, in a segment that lately is once again generating a lot of new news.

WITH WHAT WE ARE SEEING, this has been quite a long road, but finally Ethereum 2.0 is currently very close to being a reality as such. The major upgrade is basically aimed at, addressing the scalability and security of the network through a number of changes to its infrastructure, particularly; moving from a proof-of-work consensus mechanism to a proof-of-participation model.

In this aspect we must know what differences there are or exist between PoW (Proof-Of-Work) and PoS (Proof-Of-Stake).

. . .

CURRENTLY AND AS SAID BEFORE, we are in Ethereum 1.0 version which uses a consensus mechanism known as Proof-of-Work (PoW), while Ethereum 2.0 will use a consensus mechanism known as Proof-of-Stake (PoS).

WITH BLOCKCHAINS LIKE ETHEREUM, it is imperative to validate transactions in a decentralized manner. For this Ethereum, like other cryptocurrencies of the thousands that exist, currently uses the aforementioned consensus mechanism known as Proof of Work (PoW).

IN THIS SAME OPERATING SYSTEM, with the purpose of providing solutions and solving complex mathematical puzzles, miners rely on the power generated by the processing of computer hardware and thus verify new operations and transactions. The first miner to solve a puzzle adds a new transaction to the record of the total of all transactions that make up the Blockchain. Then the miners are incentivized with tokens. A whole process that, without a doubt, consumes a lot of energy.

PROOF OF STAKE (PoS) offers a big difference based on the fact that, instead of miners, validators of operations or transactions deposit cryptocurrencies in exchange for receiving the right to verify a transaction. This group of validators is selected to propose a block based on the number of cryptocurrencies they own, and how long they have held them locked up.

Another group of validators can then certify that they have seen a block. There being then enough attestors, a new block may be added to the blockchain. The validators will then be rewarded for the successful block proposition. This process is known as "forging" or "minting".

. . .

THE MAIN AND most relevant advantage of PoS is that it is much more energy efficient than PoW, as it decomposes the high-energy computational process of the consensus algorithm. It also means that high computing power is not needed to secure the Blockchain.

All of this points to the fact that Ethereum 2.0 could scale much better than the current Ethereum 1.0, with scalability being one of the main driving reasons for such an upgrade. With Ethereum 1.0 the network can effectively support a total of 30 transactions per second, but it causes heavy congestion and major inconveniences. Ethereum 2.0 on the other hand offers the possibility of 100,000 transactions per second, a considerable increase that will be achieved by fragmenting or "sharing" the chain.

The current Ethereum 1.0 configuration has a blockchain consisting of a single chain with consecutive blocks. A secure structure, but very slow and not entirely efficient. With the introduction of chain fragmentation "sharing", this Blockchain is split, allowing transactions to be handled on parallel rather than consecutive chains. This will speed up the network, and it will scale more easily.

ETHEREUM 2.0 HAS BEEN DESIGNED with security in mind as a key element. Most PoS networks, have a very small set of validators, which makes the system more centralized and in turn decreases the security of the network. Ethereum 2.0, on the other hand, requires a minimum of 16,384 validators, which makes it much more decentralized and therefore better supported in terms of security.

Audits of the security of Ethereum 2.0 code are being conducted by a group of organizations such as blockchain security firm Least Authority.

. . .

FOR ITS PART, the Ethereum Foundation is creating a multidisciplinary security team dedicated to Ethereum 2.0 to investigate what would be potential cybersecurity issues in the cryptocurrency. In a tweet, Ethereum 2.0 researcher Justin Drake stated that the research includes "fuzzing, bounty hunting, paging service, cryptoeconomic modeling, applied cryptanalysis, formal verification."

UPGRADING to Ethereum 2.0

ETHEREUM 2.0 IS TRANSITING the road to release, according to a developer of the project, but what will the future hold for such an ambitious project?

Via a post on his Twitter social network, @Vitalik.

ETH Ethereum co-founder Vitálik Buterin traced the routing detailing how the next five to ten years could turn out for Ethereum 2.0. He expresses that in the last two years he has recorded a "solid shift from blue sky research, trying to understand what is possible, to concrete research and development, thus seeking to optimize specific primitives that we know are implementable and put them into practice."

Also that the most demanding part of the challenges now "is increasingly focused on development, and the development part will only continue to grow over time."

Last June 2020, Buterin noted that Ethereum 2.0 will have to rely on current scaling methods, such as ZK Rollups, for at least two years before performing chain segmentation.

MARKET IMPACT FOLLOWING the release of Ethereum 2.0 First and foremost, Ethereum's ETH and ERC-20 tokens are secure and guaranteed. The new update will only make an overhaul to the

Ethereum Blockchain network, leaving its cryptographic components intact. Of course, users can safely expect an impact on market prices.

As the network improves, the demand for ETH is guaranteed to increase, leading to an increase in its value. Obviously, this will depend on whether the transition goes smoothly. While it is and statistically unlikely to happen, a failure of epic proportions may deem Ethereum unviable.

IT IS ALSO BELIEVED that Ethereum 2.0 will give a substantial boost to the DeFi market to new heights. Such projects require a reliable, scalable, decentralized and 100% secure blockchain infrastructure. With the upgrade, the Ethereum blockchain will perhaps be considered an ideal option.

DECENTRALIZED DAPPS APPLICATIONS, will also gain access to performance benchmarks with relevant improvements. Although slight disruptions may occur, compatibility with Ethereum 2.0 is already a given and guaranteed.

Stage "SERENITY", Ethereum version 2.0 Ethereum 2.0 Ethereum 2.0, also known as Serenity, is touted as an enhanced version of Ethereum. Thanks to the PoS (Proof-Of-Stake) algorithm, it will be more scalable and flexible. Still, the Ethereum Foundation does not want to compromise on decentralization in order to achieve greater scalability potential. Thus, the new platform aims to find the ideal balance between the two.

TO ACHIEVE THIS, Ethereum 2.0 will implement a unique architecture called sharding, which refers to a network of parallel channels working together. Each shard will have its own set of account balances and smart contracts. The method for achieving maximum decentralization will be implemented in the final phase of the upgrade.

IN THE EARLY YEARS, Ethereum did a great job of handling the transactions of millions of users and smart contract settlement. However, the demand for Ethereum services has expanded significantly on the network, resulting in inevitable congestion.

To understand how vital Ethereum is, try to think about the fact that 96% of all DeFi projects run specifically on its platform. And with over 850,000 unique DeFi users on the platform and over one million Ethereum wallet users, it's clear that the Ethereum network is in dire need of an upgrade.

THE HIGH DEMAND also resulted in an increase in fees on Ethereum, which increased by approximately 600% from August to September 2020. In the end, the need for scalability forced Ethereum to adopt PoS (Proof-Of-Stake) instead of the current PoW (Proof-Of-Work). So, here is Ethereum 2.0.

THIS IS the most ambitious overhaul of the network to date and involves the biggest improvements in almost every aspect of the network. The main weaknesses that this revision would attack would be:

SCALABILITY

WITH FULL CERTAINTY and quite possibly the biggest challenge Ethereum faces today. Adding new nodes to the network, does not increase transaction processing capacity, since each node is going to verify each transaction. The increase in the use of the Ethereum network has led to a steady growth in time and in the cost of executing operations and other transactions.

The approach to solving these problems and resolving conflicts would be carried out on two fronts: fragmentation, in which the chain would be divided into more manageable fragments, and Off-Chain solutions, very similar to Bitcoin's Lightning Network.

SPEED AND USABILITY

ASPECT CLOSELY RELATED to the previous one, although they are not at all the same. It refers to the bottleneck introduced by the Ethereum Virtual Machine EVM (Ethereum Virtual Machine) itself, which is responsible for executing and processing the code deployed over the network and maintaining the state of the network. It is also responsible for maintaining all network metadata (block number and storage among others), account information and the execution of Smart Contracts deployed on the network.

Being immersed in all these fundamental aspects of the network, makes the Ethereum Virtual Machine EVM (Ethereum Virtual Machine) a fundamental bottleneck in the overall operation of the network. With a view to improving this response, work is underway on a solution called Ethereum-WASM, in which a new set of instructions will be defined, thus seeking an improvement in the speed, security and overall performance of the network.

PROBLEMS ETHEREUM **2.0 solves and why it is so important** .

ETHEREUM 2.0 SOLUTIONS

. . .

EVERY CONSCIOUS CHANGE is the product of an idea that seeks innovations and improvements in all aspects, always the product of a need, whether it is due to a weakness, strength or opportunity.

In the case of Ethereum we could assign these three aspects without necessarily being programmers, developers or validators, even miners. And this is due to the fact of being close to these networks that, in a self-taught or professional way, we seek to know. Let's see just one example per feature, we invite you to share the ones you consider on your part.

CHANGE BY WEAKNESS:

SCALABILITY:

- Ethereum version 1.0 has the ability to support 30 transactions per second.

- ETHEREUM VERSION 2.0 offers the ability to support 100,000 transactions per second.

CHANGE FOR STRENGTH:
Knowledge.

THE ETHEREUM PLATFORM has a multidisciplinary team of experts, professionals, programmers and developers among many other talents with solid computational knowledge; who dedicate time and effort to provide their best contributions to make Ethereum a network that allows satisfying the needs of its users and community at a global level in general.

EXCHANGE FOR OPPORTUNITY:

Security.

Ethereum 2.0 seeks to transform itself, as far as possible, as the most secure platform on the network, which is why they have left this great responsibility in the hands of Least Authority, an auditing company specializing in the area of blockchain security.

Some of the main solutions that Ethereum 2.0 will bring with it:

THE PROOF-OF-WORK (POW), such as Beacon and Casper; changing the way how to create ETH and secure the system.

SHARDING usually usually divides a large amount of database into smaller, manageable parts. This will be applied to Ethereum and will address current issues such as scalability and transaction speed, thus preventing a DApp from slowing down the network.

EWASM WILL MAKE code run faster, thus increasing the options and coding capabilities of the Ethereum Virtual Machine (EVM) Virtual Machine.

PLASMA IS one more layer that is located on top of the network and is fully capable of handling large amounts of transactions. It could even be compared to Bitcoin's Lightening Network for Ethereum.

• • •

RAIDEN, similar to Plasma, is a timely more off-chain scaling solution. So it could be seen as an imitation of Bitcoin's Lightning Network.

Some differences between PoS (Proff-Of-Stake) and PoW (Proof-Of-Work) The concept behind the Proof-of-Stake and Proof-of-Work consensus mechanisms boils down to how network participants, called nodes, are validating transactions on their respective blockchains and maintaining the normal state of the platform.

POW (PROOF-OF-WORK), which was first introduced by Bitcoin in 2008 (in fact, the concept of PoW was developed long before Bitcoin), nodes can become so-called miners to validate new Mempool transactions by solving complex mathematical puzzles. Participants must devote computational power to win the competition and earn the right to validate the next block. In return for their efforts, miners receive a reward in the form of Bitcoin or newly generated cryptocurrencies that use the PoW (Proof-Of-Work) consensus.

PoS (Proof-Of-Stake) came later as an alternative to PoW (Proof-Of-Work), as it attempted to solve Bitcoin's main problems related to scalability and energy consumption, among others.

UNLIKE POW (PROOF-OF-WORK) BLOCKCHAIN, PoS (Proof-Of-Stake) networks do not involve miners, as most of these projects are launched with previously mined tokens. The validation of new blocks in PoS systems is known as "forging". While validators are the nodes involved in the creation of the block.

Then, to become a validator, nodes must block a part of the native token. Generally, the more tokens they bet, the higher the chance of becoming the next validator. The same approach will be applied in the next Ethereum 2.0 update.

. . .

LET'S not forget that Ethereum 2.0 is an update to the Ethereum network that has been expected for some time now, a version that promises significant improvements in functionality and network experience as a whole, and that among its most notable improvements are the transition to Proof-Of-Stake (PoS), "shard chains" and a new Blockchain at the base that will be or is referred to as "Beacon Chain".

All this development and much more is planned to be rolled out gradually through a carefully planned roadmap, in fact; published by Vitálik Buterin himself on his official Twitter account, @Vitalik.ETH, using the hashtag #ETH2.

FASCINATING NEW PROJECTS are being built on Ethereum: microgrids, electric vehicle charging stations, cryptocurrencies, home mortgages, health care records, voting networks and much more.

All these alternatives are possible thanks to the Ethereum Virtual Machine Ethereum Virtual Machine (EVM). An intelligent supercomputer developed with full dedication, following a high-level programming process. The computer is not physical, as its name suggests. It is distributed as software on the Ethereum blockchain and developers can access it (software) freely.

THE ETHEREUM VIRTUAL Machine Ethereum Virtual Machine (EVM) is smarter than any average computer because it develops what we also know as "Turing complete". The renowned Turing complete programming language is theoretically capable of expressing each and every task that can be performed by computers as we know them.

The implications of this are staggering. Ethereum Virtual Machine Ethereum Virtual Machine (EVM) uses its native programming language called Solidity, which is capable of executing any type of script. "Normal" computers are only capable of running scripts coded by the computer manufacturers.

. . .

ETHEREUM'S IMPORTANCE is overshadowed by its price actions, and we are likely to be surprised in the future how much can be done with it. It's like the beginning of the Internet, where people really didn't know what it would become.

IN THE SAME WAY, Ethereum is the Internet of Money, where everything is transparent and open to everyone, an opportunity to "be and do more than you are," Louis Walls.

Ethereum is here to stay, and the long-awaited upgrade to Ethereum 2.0 is expected to further mitigate scalability challenges and guide the platform towards mass adoption, driving decentralized finance and its potential for financial inclusion.

THE BEACONCHAIN

WITH CHAINS of shards working in parallel, one thing must be ensured; and that is that they all stay in sync with each other. The BeaconChain takes care of such synchronization and provides consensus to all shard chains running in parallel.

THE BEACONCHAIN IS a new Blockchain that plays a central role in Ethereum 2.0. Without it, information exchange between shards could not be possible and scalability would be non-existent. For this reason, it has been said that it will be the first feature shipped on the road to Ethereum 2.0. But this is just the tip of the iceberg, as they say.

Given that Ethereum is one of the most popular cryptocurrencies in the world, there are a number of very important details regarding

ETHEREUM IN A NUTSHELL 131

what Ethereum 2.0 truly represents and the impact it will have on the "crypto-verse" and its entirety.

As we already know Ethereum 2.0 is a major upgrade to the Ethereum network for a number of reasons, primarily and especially when it comes to scalability. Without the new Proof-Of-Work (PoS) features, shard chains and the BeaconChain, Ethereum could eventually become unsustainable and would cease to be the leading Smart Contracts smart contracts platform in the global crypto ecosystem.

THE IMPLEMENTATION and execution of Eth2 will take some time, as long as it takes and may even take longer than expected. The good news is that it is already underway and its own Ethereum developers are dedicated to seeing it through with all their might.

WHAT WILL THE BEACONCHAIN DO?

Think of BeaconChain as a big lighthouse rising above a blue sea of transaction data. It is constantly scanning, validating, collecting votes and doling out rewards to validators who correctly certify blocks, deducting bounties for those who are offline and clipping ETH from malicious actors.

You can still send ETH to a friend, exchange tokens on Meta-Mask or Uniswap, play with your Axies, create NFTs on Mintbase and produce a farm on your favorite DeFi protocol. Ethereum as you know it is still active and fully functional, and will remain so until it merges with the new Eth2 blockchain and becomes a separate shard. In the meantime, a massive new structure is being built alongside Ethereum.

THE CORE of this structure is the BeaconChain, which reforms the consensus model from Proof of Work to Proof of Participation. The BeaconChain is now live, and at the time of writing, 20 epochs (an epoch is 6.4 minutes long, and each epoch contains 32 validators randomly assigned to propose a block in each slot).

THE BEACONCHAIN IS the coordination mechanism for the new network, responsible for creating new blocks, making sure those new blocks are valid, and rewarding validators with ETH for keeping the network secure. Proof of Stake has long been part of Ethereum's roadmap and addresses some of the weaknesses of Proof of Work blockchains, such as accessibility, centralization and scalability.

Instead of miners expending energy to validate blocks, randomly selected validators (each with their 32 ETH share) propose new blocks, which are voted on by other validators. Each block includes a source of randomness, which is mixed with the other random data of the time.

THE BEACONCHAIN IS the foundation of Ethereum's future. It implements Proof of Stake instead of Proof of Work as its governance mechanism, and supports scalability and security to sustain Ethereum for years to come.

THIS IS what went live on December 1. It was called "proof of stake." It is our high-value demonstration that securing a global, massively distributed, permissionless network in this way is practical and effective. BeaconChain still doesn't do much more than run on its own, and we'll get to that, but it is nonetheless the most challenging product in the Ethereum 2.0 project.

The BeaconChain already dwarfs any other Proof of Stake system. More than two million ETH, worth $1.5 billion, have been committed to the deposit contract. This represents over forty-six thousand currently active validators, with another twenty thousand in a three-week queue to join. And deposit rates show no signs of slowing. It won't be many days before 2% of the total ETH supply is locked into the deposit contract. This is an immense vote of confidence from 4,000 unique depositors and thousands more who made deposits through participation services.

So far, bettors' confidence has been well placed. It's still early days, but BeaconChain has run smoothly to date, with around 99% participation (a key metric of the network's status) and not a single problem or incident.

Hundreds of people participated in the design and build of BeaconChain over the past two and a half years. It has been a massively open community project, led by the Ethereum Foundation, implemented by customer development teams and supported by a huge and diverse group of contributors.

ETHEREUM 2.0 END OF MINING?

THAT'S the question many are asking and continue to ask. It has long been projected that cryptocurrencies, in the current model, are unsustainable, and Ethereum 2.0 is a further confirmation of this, and that a change in the model used for the management of Blockchains, a key and main element of them and of the new economic pattern that has emerged from the hand of finchech, but which is also being associated with the processes of traditional financial and commercial entities, is necessary, as well as imminent.

The difficulty that many of us are considering, and which we have been hearing and talking about for a long time, is the processing capacity, and the consequent energy consumption, which is already necessary to mine virtual currencies.

Ten years ago, currency mining was within the reach of the vast majority, but the growing complexity of the blocks to be mined has been increasing substantially, and with it the processing capacity required for this purpose. And, additionally, shooting up the price of hardware that, such as graphics cards, are especially useful for this purpose. Ethereum 2.0 is going to be a big change in this regard.

THE KEY to Ethereum 2.0 is that unlike its version 1.0, and in the same way that many other cryptocurrencies do, it changes the afore-mentioned consensus system. A change that will produce several improvements in the operation of this currency, improving the volume of transactions that the network can support simultaneously, in addition to improving the security of transactions thanks to the security audit and the increase of validators and, according to its creators, a significant growth in its value.

One of the aspects mentioned by its creators is the efficiency that Ethereum 2.0 will bring, an efficiency in terms of operations, of course, but which also has to do with the way in which new coins are obtained. And is that the proof-of-work model does not require users to perform, with their hardware, the complex operations necessary to validate operations, a process in which they obtain cryptocurrencies.

Instead, and with this new model, it is the transaction validators who are responsible for concluding whether a block is valid or not, a process for which a decentralized network of no less than 16,384 validators will be used.

THE CRYPTOCURRENCY that the user gets as a reward for being the first to validate a block disappears with this model, and the addi-tional advantage is that the operation of the proof-of-stake model is not only distributed, but it is much more efficient in terms of resource and, therefore, energy consumption, thus extending its sustainability in the medium and long term.

Ethereum 2.0, with this change of model, takes a step that, sooner or later, we will surely also see in other cryptocurrencies such as Bitcoin. And, related to the above, this may also put an end to the speculative business that has been generated around graphics cards, highly coveted by cryptocurrency miners for their capacity in terms of floating point calculation, something very valuable in proof-of-work processes.

When the migration to Ethereum 2.0 is complete, and even more so when other cryptocurrencies make this leap, we will likely see a noticeable increase in the availability of the latest generation of graphics cards on the market.

THE TRANSITION to the Proof-of-Stake PoS (Proof-Of-Stake) algorithm, will change mining approaches, so it is likely that most miners will leave the market. Since ETH is the most popular currency for domestic mining, the impact will be palpable.

AS A RESULT, ETH miners will have the option of selling their equipment to start gambling or switching to other networks and mining coins that don't plan major changes to their protocols. But the reality is that most miners will likely pull the plug and the remaining market participants will start betting their assets.

Consequently, the network will abandon the PoS (Proof-Of-Work) proof-of-work consensus algorithm, leaving Ether miners with very few options. Since their equipment will become obsolete, they will be forced to start mining altcoins or recertify as ETH gamblers.

FROM THE ABOVE, the relevance of miners to the new version when it launches will be very low. A more vital question is what the overall relevance of miners will be afterwards.

THE RELEASE of Ethereum 2.0 will not completely render the previous version useless from the start. Ethereum 1.0 will continue to function normally, but this would not undermine the established plans. The intention of Ethereum 1.0 is to effectively become the first Ethereum 2.0 shard when Phase 1 launches. Until then, the Ethereum 1.0 blockchain will continue as it is now and undergo enhancements to eventually become an Ethereum 2.0 shard.

DEAR READER, digital currencies have created quite a stir ever since the prices of certain types of cryptocurrencies suddenly went up. As we see, this has become a new trend in the investment world for real and fair reasons. People who invested in them have benefited in unimaginable ways.

UNDERSTANDING **the importance of cryptocurrencies and secure money management .**
Why have cryptocurrencies become so popular and are trending in the crypto-asset world?

THIS IS another question that many of us also ask ourselves, and we are always curious and eager to know a little more. Let us share some aspects that, based on the importance that cryptocurrencies represent today, will provide us with an interesting answer.

A CRYPTOCURRENCY IS a digital currency that uses crypto-graphic encryption to generate money and verify transactions. In a more technical term, it is a peer-to-peer encrypted virtual currency made up of codes and is like any other medium of exchange such as dollars, pounds and euros, but in this aspect, exchanges make use of encrypted details and exchange digital tokens in a distributed and decentralized manner, a quality of great value; and these tokens can be traded at market rates.

Until the invention of cryptocurrency, it was impossible for two parties to transact electronically without employing the service of a third party or trusted intermediary. The reason was the "double-spending" problem, which plagued all attempts to create electronic cash since the dawn of the Internet.

HERE ARE the reasons why cryptocurrencies are really important.

- CRYPTOCURRENCIES ARE one of the safest and most trusted types of digital currency that people prefer today. In a world where insecurity abounds, we all need to trade in the most trustworthy way possible. Cryptocurrencies provide us with that security that makes them an important source of investment now and also in the future.

- ANOTHER REASON why cryptocurrencies have become extremely in demand is because of their policies. You really don't need to deal with a third party when it comes to cryptocurrencies. This gives people a sense of peace of mind and security. The fact that cryptocurrencies are digital currencies alleviates the need for a third party. You can transact no matter where you are.

- CRYPTOCURRENCIES ARE a low-cost means of transaction. You do not need to shell out money to exchange digital currencies. All you need to be able to transact is your cell phone or computer and a basic knowledge of cryptocurrencies.

- MOST DIGITAL CURRENCIES have to pay for transactions. In the case of cryptocurrencies, you don't really need to pay for transactions. The reason is that the people who mine the cryptocurrencies, called miners; get their compensation from the network itself.

. . .

- YOU CAN STORE your cryptocurrencies in a secure wallet. Cryptocurrencies give you the option of storing your money in two types of wallets that can be easily transferred to your account. And the wallets are free of charge in order to store your digital currencies.

- FOR MOST PEOPLE, privacy is the top priority. When trading cryptocurrencies, you can expect your transactions to be highly confidential. You can conduct your transactions and be anonymous.

- THE AMOUNT of money you want to invest depends entirely on whether cryptocurrencies give you the freedom to buy them in fractions as well. If you think a Bitcoin or an Ether is too expensive, you can split it and buy half or a third. This reduces the cost to you and doesn't require you to spend outside the limits. With a cryptocurrency converter, you can find out the price of any cryptocurrency in your country's currency and invest accordingly.

- SINCE CRYPTOCURRENCY SENDERS and recipients do not transfer money directly to credit cards, you do not need to share your documents with third parties. This helps you avoid identity theft. You decide what information you want to share with the merchant if something makes you hesitate.

- GET the full autonomy you're looking for. When it comes to cryptocurrencies, there is no third party involved to demand any fees or money. You are the only person managing your account.

SEVEN

GENERATING PASSIVE INCOME WITH ETHEREUM AND OTHER CRYPTOCURRENCIES

As you may have noticed throughout the development of the book, there are currently several ways to generate money with cryptocurrencies, there are many opportunities. While there are some that are more risky (and depend on your ability) such as trading, DeFi platforms, etc, there are others that are more recommended and less risky, such as making Hodl of a cryptocurrency and wait for its price to rise, although this earning model is absolutely passive, as it is a long-term strategy, we have other strategies that can also help you generate passive income, as is the strategy that I will present below.

This strategy has existed for many years, is widely used by banks today, although in a higher percentage of profit, this generate interest with your assets.

In the world of cryptocurrencies this modality already exists and is led by one of the most reliable companies in the environment: BlockFi, which is backed by the Gemini exchange and people as recognized in the environment as Anthony Pompliano.

BlockFi allows us to transfer our funds to the platform and generate an annual interest that goes from 6% (for cryptocurrencies such as Bitcoin) or almost 10% with stablecoins (which are cryptocurrencies that are 1 to 1 with the dollar, such as USDT and USDC to name a few).

IF YOU ARE **interested in this modality, you can open a BlockFi account at the following link and earn $250 of Bitcoin for free:**

GET your BONUS on BlockFi here

IN CASE you are reading this book in the printed version you can scan the following QR code with your cell phone:

EIGHT

THE MOST IMPORTANT THINGS TO KEEP IN MIND WITH ETHEREUM

To conclude this book, I would like to thank you for taking the time to read it, I wanted to clarify a few things before finishing.

Many people have tried dabbling in cryptocurrencies, some with success others with moderate results, but all with results in the end, the important thing is that you keep in mind that the cryptocurrency market is a highly manipulated market, which is why I recommend that you always pay attention to the indicators that you can see in TradingView, see the signals it sends you, continue learning about trading, if you are interested you can dedicate yourself to them, but if not you can dedicate yourself to do HODL (the meaning of this within the Cryptocurrencies is related to buy coins when there is a significant decline (for example if Bitcoin is at $58000 and falls to $36500 there is where you buy and go buying as it falls, never when it goes up, this is known as Dollar Cost Averaging is a strategy widely used in the trading environment) and keep those cryptocurrencies for years until they double, triple or quadruple their value, it is not uncommon in the environment, as well have done those early adopters who bought Bitcoin when it was worth $0.006 cents, did HODL for 14 years and when Bitcoin reached its all-time high of $20,000 dollars in 2017 and $60,000 in 2021, sold everything and became millionaires. But as always, choose the method you like best and follow it at your own risk.

FINALLY, I would like to know your comments to continue to nurture this book and to help many more people, for them would you help us by leaving a review of this book, in order to continue providing great books to you, my readers, which I appreciate very much.

LINKS **for you**

Check crypto prices here:
https://coinmarketcap.com/
Get free Bitcoin:
Get free bitcoin here
Get your BlockFi bonus here:
https://blockfi.com/?ref=76971ae9

Trading crypto:

Binance

Bitmex

Buy Crypto:

Coinbase

CEX.IO

Changally

Localbitcoins

Donde guardar tus criptomonedas:

Get the Trezor Model T here

Get the Trezor Model ONE here

Get a Ledger Nano S here

More trading tools at:
www.TradingView.com

www.ingramcontent.com/pod-product-compliance
Lightning Source LLC
Chambersburg PA
CBHW030522210326
41597CB00013B/1003